GUSTAVE LANGENUS

COMPLETE METHOD

for the

CLARINET

IN THREE PARTS

Book I

Published in 2019 by Allegro Editions

Complete Method for the Clarinet [1]
ISBN: 978-1-9748-9963-0 (paperback)

Cover design by Kaitlyn Whitaker

Cover image: "Close Up Detail of a Woodwind Clarinet"
by Mark Yuill courtesy of Shutterstock;
"Music Sheet" by Danielo courtesy of Shutterstock

ALLEGRO EDITIONS

TABLE OF CONTENTS

Table of Contents	II
Historical Note	III
Introduction. To the Beginner-the Advanced player,-the Teacher	IV, V
Different parts of the Clarinet	VI
Position of the Body, Hands and Fingers	VII
The Embouchure	VIII
Action of the Tongue	IX
Breathing	=
Tone	X
Preliminary Remarks	=
On Squeaks	=
How to Practice	=
Chart of Fingering	XI
Preliminary Studies .... FIRST BOOK	1
Sustained Tones	2
Studies on Intervals	3
Studies in the Clarion Register	4
Studies between the Chalumeau and Clarion Registers	5-6
Rhythmic Studies in 2/4, 3/4 and 4/4 time	7
Duos *By KLOSÉ and BERR*	8
Staccato Studies	9-10
Studies on Intervals	11
Studies for the High B and C	12
Articulation Studies	13
Rhythmic Studies	14
Studies for F♯ Fingerings .... SECOND BOOK	15-16
Duos *By G.L.*	17
Rhythmic Studies Duos *By G.L.*	18
Duos Dotted Notes *By BERR*	19
On Rhythm and Syncopation Duos *By G.L.*	20-23
Studies for the High D	24-25
Rhythmic Studies in 3/8 time	26
Studies for the B♭ Fingerings	27-28
Rhythmic Studies in 6/8 time Duos *By G.L.*	29-30
Technical Exercises .... THIRD BOOK	31
Studies for the C♯-D♭ Fingerings	32-33
On Forte-Piano, Crescendo and Diminuendo	34-36
Theme and Variations, Duo	37-39
Studies for the E♭-D♯ Fingerings, Also High F	40-42
Duos *By DANCLA, BERR*	43-44
Technical Studies	45-46
Studies for the G♯-A♭ Fingerings, Also for Key D. FOURTH BOOK	47-49
Technical Studies	50
Studies of Crescendi and Diminueni	51
Marks of Expression	52
Studies in Dynamics	=
On Expression	53
Duos *By G.L. and KLOSÉ*	54-55
Technical Studies	56-57
Duos *By BERR, HANDEL, G.L., PLEYEL, SPOHR, BERR*	58-62
Syncopation Studies	63
Duos *By L. MOZART, CAMPAGNOLI*	64
On Distorted Rhythms .... FIFTH BOOK	65
Duos *By G.L.*	66
Forte-Piano Studies	67
Sforzando and Accents	68
Accented eighth notes	69
Dotted notes	69
Legato Staccato	=
Duos *By BERR, MAZAS, WEBER, BERR, DE BERIOT*	70-73
Technical Studies *By CAMPAGNOLI, DANCLA, A.B. BRUNI*	74-77
Studies for the High F♯ and G Fingerings	78
Scale Studies	79-80
Chromatic Scale Studies	81
Technical Studies *By KREUTZER, GRIEG*	82
Duos *By BERR, SPOHR*	83-86
Musical Terms	87-88

Historical Note

The word "Clarinet" or, as the older spelling has it, "Clarionet," is probably the diminutive of "Clarion," a high trumpet, which instrument the Clarinet displaced in military music when it first came into general use.

Little is known of the early history of Clarinet making. Previous to 1700 it was called Chalumeau and had a very limited and uncertain range — from F below to B♭ in the staff — and seems to have been more of a toy than a musical instrument.

About 1700, Christopher Denner, a manufacturer of musical instruments at Nuremberg, by increasing the length of the B♭ sound hole, added the notes from C, third space, to E above the staff. Excepting for the low E, and the B natural, third line, it now had a range of three octaves.

It is not known who, between 1700 and 1750, added the B-E key, but at about this time 1750, Barthold Fritz is credited with adding the F sharp-C sharp key, and Joseph Beer the A flat - E flat key.

From then, owing to its natural beauty and perfect blending quality of tone, the Clarinet took an important place in ensemble playing.

Xavier Lefebvre added the C sharp-G sharp key in 1805, and in 1814 Iwan Muller brought out the 13 keyed Clarinet. This instrument was in good tune throughout, and its smoothness of tone and technical possibilities surpassed all previous Clarinets. However, the contemporaries of Muller thought his "new" system too complicated, and in spite of the financial assistances of a banker, Muller was compelled to wind up his business and leave Paris.

In 1839, L. A. Buffet exhibited in Paris, a Clarinet to which was applied the mechanical system Boehm had applied to the Piccolo and Flute, but the patent for this instrument was not issued until 1844, Buffet an Klosé are equally credited with having brought the so-called Boehm system Clarinet to its present state of efficiency.

While there are many different systems of Clarinets advertised, I do not think there has been any great progress made in Clarinet manufacture since the invention of the 17 keyed, 6 ring Boehm system Clarinet; and I know that its possibilities are ample, while music remains in its present stage of development.

INTRODUCTION
TO THE BEGINNER

It is very difficult to learn the Clarinet by self-tuition; therefore, in order to avoid acquiring wrong habits, secure the services of the best teacher in your vicinity.

Reading music is a mathematical accomplishment; interpreting it on an instrument is a different study. For that reason it is advisable for you to know the rudiments of music and be able to read music tolerably well before taking up any instrument. What you cannot read you cannot play; hence, the necessity of constantly studying music reading apart of the instrument in order to keep abreast of your technic. If your teacher is compelled to stop you frequently telling you that you read wrong notes or that your rhythm is faulty, then you are wasting his time and he necessarily must give you lessons in elementary music reading, whereas, he ought to be able to give all his attention to teaching you clarinet-playing.

In the first part of this Method, many points about clarinet-playing are explained which a cursory reading will not disclose. Therefore, do not just read it over but study it over carefully, together with the additional annotations of your teacher. Unless sufficient attention is given to the little things, "unconsidered trifles", then mediocrity results. Many clarinet players have technic without a good tone; others, may have technic and tone but cannot phrase well; and still others seem to have them all and yet do not play in tune, or lack life in their playing; their interpretation is like a monotonous recitation. The clarinetist, worthy of the name, must have them all, and it is only by learning the little details that he can become proficient on his instrument.

TO THE ADVANCED PLAYER

Quite a number of good clarinet-players who took a short intensive course with me, were at first somewhat disappointed because I made them go through certain studies in Part 1. I have two reasons for making them do so; the first is because in most cases they have a disregard for apparently easy studies, such as Nos. 8, 16 etc. Yet, when one has to play at a Symphony Concert a similar pasage as a solo, one soon finds out that it is not so easy, especially, when one realizes that over three thousand people are listening to you. Draw a horizontal line and see how difficult it is to make it perfectly straight without the aid of a ruler. The same applies to the tone, to have that straight without a waver, or making an even crescendo and diminuendo, those are not easy accomplishments. I know of many a fine performer who prefers to play the Cadenza in Tchaikowsky's Suite "Mozartiana" to some of the following "simple" solos:

However, the advanced student soon discovers the importance of those "trifles" and feels so much better equipped afterward.

The second reason of going through certain studies of Part 1, is that the player will have acquired a solid foundation which he can use effectively with his prospective pupils. He also usually appreciates the fact that the REMARKS contained in Part 1 and 2, are verbal suggestions received from my esteemed teachers Poncelet and Hanon of the Brussels' Conservatoire, besides being a summary of my own experience of twenty years Orchestra and Chamber music playing — whatever that may be worth.

The best advice I can give the ambitious player is to imagine that an audience is listening to him when he practices, and this for a good psychological reason.

TO THE TEACHER

When I set about to write this Method for Clarinet seven years ago, it was not vanity that prompted me to do so. Until then I had taught from the Methods, by Berr, Klosé and Baermann who, I hasten to add, were masters in melodic writing for the Clarinet, unsurpassed to this day. However, from the teacher's point of view, I had great difficulty is selecting suitable and graded material for the beginner in particular. From Study 1, I had to pass over several pages to pick up the next step he could safely tred, and then back again to Study No. 2, and so forth, jumping from one page to another, in an attempt to bridge the different problems. The task was not easy. Therefore, I ventured to write a Method, trying to avoid the obstacles, contained in the other Methods, which handicapped me as a teacher and, worse yet, the pupil. In consequence I have endeavoured to link the studies so that one difficulty is taken up at a time. Figuratively speaking, I have tried to grade a road without any sharp curves or sudden steep inclines. To attain my objective, and for making the work of the pupil more interesting, I borrowed liberally compositions from such masters as Berr, De Beriot, Campagnoli, Handel, Klose, Mazas, Mozart, Pleyel, Spohr and others.

However since I brought out the first edition of this work, I have not been entirely satisfied, Also, I have learned quite a few things. For instance, instead of starting the beginner with the preliminary studies with the open G, repeating the same note by tongue action, I found that I could get better results from a beginner by giving him the first note of E on the first line. This note is just as easy to emit as the open G, with the advantage that the pupil can steady his embouchure better as he has two fingers helping him to support the Clarinet, besides the thumbrest. I also discovered that tongueing was premature at this stage and the aspirating of the first note much more preferable, avoiding thereby, over pressure between the teeth and lower lip. For the first lessons I usually let the beginner concentrate on the "feeling" of his fingers on the tone holes, giving him free hand as to the rhythm. Only after he has played to the end of study No. 6, do I make him repeat everything in exact time. Some other important changes are, for instance, the preliminary studies on page 18 to Study 79, to acquire the feeling of the exact value of the dotted eighth notes followed by a sixteenth note contained in studies 79 and 80. I have also added a number of rhythmic studies, for I found many of my pupils weak in that respect.

In concluding I wish to thank the teachers and soloists that have pointed out some errors in the first edition and offered suggestions. It will give me much pleasure to receive further helpful criticisms which will tend to make the next edition of this Method more complete yet.

G. LANGENUS

Different Parts of the Clarinet

The Clarinet consists generally of five pieces: 1-mouthpiece; 2-barrel; 3-upper or left hand joint; 4-lower or right hand joint; 5-bell. (See Fig. 1)

Fig. 1

The Mouthpiece

The mouthpiece is the most important part of the Clarinet. It is preferable to have a good mouthpiece and an inferior instrument than the contrary. Mouthpieces are made of different materials. Specially prepared hard rod rubber is used by the best mouthpiece makers; it is more expensive than the soft cast rubber mouthpieces, but the former will outlast the latter many times. Crystal is also used to a certain extent but a good one is seldom found on account that it is very difficult to make it with the right proportions. It also has the disadvantage of the saliva adhering to it like vapor, making the tone fuzzy when playing very softly; contrarily, the saliva runs freely down on ebonite.

Fig. 2

The Lay

The lay is that part of the mouthpiece on which the reed lies. It is almost level, except near the tip, where the two sides slope away from the reed, leaving a slight opening for the reed to vibrate upon. This opening varies in different facings. I use and recommend what is commonly called the French lay, as indicated by the heavy line on figure 2. The dotted lines represent the varieties of German lays.

The Reed and Ligature

The reed is a thin piece of cane cut from a certain grass, called by botanists, Arundo Sativa. It is grown on the Mediterranean coast. It plays an important part in tone production and great care should be exercised in its selection. The reed must not be so hard as to cause effort in playing. Ease and naturalness are the desiderata to be held in view; those are only to be obtained with a good mouthpiece and a good reed. The ligature secures the reed to the mouthpiece. The reed is placed centrally and its point must not overlap the tip of the mouthpiece. (See Fig. 3) A cap is used to protect the reed.

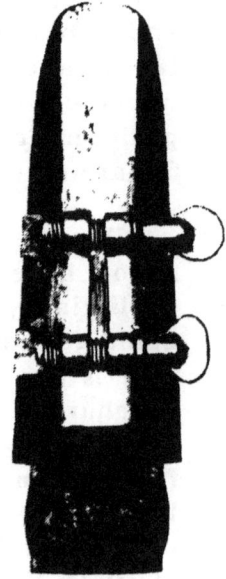

Fig. 3

Position of the Body, Hands and Fingers

Some effort should be expended in acquiring a graceful and easy bearing while playing the Clarinet. If standing the weight of the body should rest on the left foot, and the right foot be brought a little forward. When seated the position of the feet is of less importance. The head may be inclined downward slightly, but the shoulders must, at all times, be held well back, to allow the lungs full play. The elbows are to be kept in an unstrained, natural position, near the body.

The Clarinet should be held at an angle of about forty degrees from the body. The left hand is placed on the upper joint, the right hand on the lower.

The weight of the instrument is supported by the right hand thumb, using for this purpose the thumb rest on the lower joint.

Do not strike the tone holes, with the very tips of the fingers, like on the Piano or Violin. The fingers should be bent only slightly, like a gentle curve, (see accompanying illustrations) with the points of the fingers overlapping the holes about one eighth of an inch. This will insure a perfect covering. When in action the fingers should not be raised more than an inch above the tone holes or keys. The upward motion must be as swift as the downward one. Beginners are apt to cramp the fingers on the tone holes; needless to say this is bad. The fingers must be independently agile and free from stiffness.

The Embouchure

Embouchure is a much abused French word which, literally translated, means "inmouthing." Applied to the Clarinet it denotes the manner in which the mouthpiece is held in the mouth with the aid of lips and teeth. (On Brass-instruments the mouthpiece is called embouchure.)

In this country there are four distinct embouchures used among the different players:
1. Both lips drawn over teeth, reed resting against upper lip.
2. Both lips drawn over teeth, reed resting upon lower lip.
3. Reed resting upon lower lip, upper teeth pressing mouthpiece about an inch from the point.
4. Reed resting upon lower lip, upper teeth, or tooth, resting one third of an inch from the point of mouthpiece.

The first belongs to the very old Italian School of Clarinet Playing and is fast becoming obsolete.

The second is taught in the French Schools, and is supported by some eminent performers. In most cases, this embouchure requires a very soft reed, with the result that the pitch of the instrument sharpens considerably in *piano* passages, and flattens in *forte*, requiring continual and great effort to play in tune.

The third belongs to the German School. It requires a long lay and hard lip pressure. The embouchure is not at all suitable for the Boehm Clarinet, as it makes the tone a little coarse, thereby preventing it from blending well with the Oboe, the Flute, and other wind and string instruments. It is also extremely difficult to play with this embouchure as delicately as the aforementioned instruments, yet modern interpretation demands it from the Clarinet.

I use and recommend the fourth embouchure, wich is almost the same as the French, except that the upper teeth are allowed to touch the mouthpiece instead of being enveloped by the upper lip. With this embouchure a slightly harder reed is used, insuring a greater equilibrium of pitch, yet the same delicacy of tone, as secured by the use of the French embouchure. A detailed description of this embouchure follows:

1_ The lower lip is slightly drawn over the teeth.
2_ Let the reed rest on the rim of the lower lip about half an inch from the tip.
3_ The point of the reed must be free from any contact with lip or tongue for at least a quarter of an inch in order to vibrate freely against the lay.
4_ The upper teeth_or inner corner of one central tooth_rest (not press) on the mouthpiece, not over half an inch from the point.
5_ The lips and especially the corners of the mouth must be compressed inwardly around the mouthpiece like an elastic band.

Special Recommendations

Hold the mouthpiece steady, do not allow the fingers to push it out of position. If the air escapes from the sides of the lips it means that rule No. 5 (See above paragraph) is not faithfully followed. Puffing out of cheeks looks abominably. To get the high notes contract the throat a little more than for the lower notes, using also a slightly lower lip pressure upon the reed by bringing the jaw out a little.

If the tone is not satisfactory, change the embouchure ever so little; a sixteenth of an inch more or less freedom of the reed within the mouth often leads to a remarkable improvement.

Never start a tone without getting the saliva off the reed through suction.

The right hand thumb not only stabilizes the holding of the Clarinet, but it also helps greatly the tone quality if the pressure of the thumb is upwards.

Action of the Tongue

A reed is a vibrating body which is set in motion by the air. It suffices to touch it ever so lightly at its thin edge with the tongue and no sound will be forthcoming, though the air continues to enter into the instrument. The understanding of the foregoing statement is very important. Formerly, I advocated the action of the tongue closing up the opening between the reed and the lay; others taught the use of syllables, such as "tu" or "tah" for tongueing; but in time, I have found it better to touch the reed ever so little, and with gratifying results.

In order to play staccato in this manner, I recommend that the tip of the tongue be curved downward and always remain in that position when playing. Consequently, the reed is touched by that part of the tongue about a fourth of an inch from its end. Thus the reed is struck about a sixteenth of an inch below its thin edge. The tongue must be hard, muscular-like, when playing quick staccato passages, fp or sf, touching the reed as lightly as possible. For staccato-legato playing the tongue is in a relaxed position. Under no circumstances should the action of the tongue be such as to prevent the air from entering the instrument. In other words, the tongue merely stops the vibrating of the reed for the time being.

Note: The beginner should not heed the above until he gets to Study 36.

Breathing

Correct breathing is as important to the wind instrumentalist as to the singer. The breath and reed bear the same relationship as to the bow and string of the Violin. Sufficient attention has not been given to breathing by Clarinet players as a whole, and I strongly advise the reading of authoritative books on voice culture, as the breathing methods thaught therein are equally valuable for the clarinetist.

There are three methods of breathing generally taught: the costal, the abdominal and the clavicular. Each requires a concentrated effort on the part of the player: the first to expand the ribs, the second to force the diaphragm out and down, the third to force the collar-bone and shoulder-blades up and out.

While many teachers have taught the different methods, I believe a combination of the three, as advocated by Dr. Frank E. Miller, to be the best. He says in "The Voice:" "The correct method combines the three — adds to the inflation of the central and upper parts of the lungs accomplished by costal breathing, the inflation of the lower part accomplished in diaphragmatic breathing and of the extreme upper part accomplished in clavicular breathing. In other words, the correct method inflates the whole of the lungs and creates a cavity large enough to accommodate them."

Some teachers of wind instruments recommend the abdominal, or diaphragmatic, breathing method exclusively. I cannot agree with them.

Watch a healthy child sleeping, and pattern your breathing thereby.

There must be no noticeable effort attached to breathing. Ease and naturalness are ends to be sought.

Except when it is necessary to take a quick breath, clarinetists should take breath through the nostrils.

When taking-in breath the purpose held in view should be, to expand the ribs, to lower the diaphragm and raise the clavicle. This makes the most room in the lung chamber, and the whole idea is to get in as much air with as little effort as possible.

In playing care must be taken about wasting breath from the sides of the mouth. Air must not escape from the nostrils, as it has a disagreeable and nasal effect on the tone.

It is a very usual thing for clarinetists to use more air than is necessary for tone production. The amount of air taken in should be regulated by the length of the phrase to be played. For a passage of two measures the player needs less breath than for eight. Therefore take less.

It is advisable to take breathing exercises daily before breakfast. Stand with the back and head touching a wall. Take breath slowly through the nostrils until the lungs are filled. Pause five seconds and let the air escape slowly through the mouth.

This exercise practised a few times each morning will be of the utmost service to all.

Tone

To secure a good tone on the Clarinet one must be equipped with a good instrument, a good mouthpiece and a good reed. But above all things one must play with a correct embouchure.

Everything should be sacrificed for a beautiful tone. No amount of technic, when the tone is coarse, will give such pleasure as a simple phrase played with a clear and pleasing tone quality. A beautiful voice is expected from a singer; if he does not possess this, his high notes and vocalisms do not charm, but leave us cold. The same is true of the clarinetist. No instrument can emit such a rough, disagreeable sound as the Clarinet, and, on the other hand, no wind instrument can equal it in golden tones. The tone of the lower register resembles the contralto voice in richness and mellowness, while the clarion register possesses the sweet and tender qualities of the soprano.

What is called a vibrating tone, caused by the glottis, or throat action, should be studiously avoided; it is extremely obnoxious on any wind instrument.

The tone of the Clarinet should be pure, clear and steady; only when playing very loudly, or when playing the notes of the third register, should the tone be allowed to vibrate a little to give warmth to the playing, and to cover the harshness of the high notes.

Always remember that the tone is of supreme importance, and let it have the first consideration in all your studies.

Preliminary Remarks

Do not consult the Chart of Fingering at first, except to memorize the letters given to the keys on the Clarinet as marked on the diagram. This will save time later when reference is made to any particular fingering. The six finger holes on the upper side of the Clarinet are designated by little circles, i, e., ○ or ●. When black, it denotes that the finger must cover the hole; when white, that the hole must be left open. A horizontal line separates the left from the right hand fingers (see ill.) The letter found adjacent to circles denotes which key must be taken. The letter is placed in such a manner that is shows by which finger the key must be manipulated with. The X indicates that the thumb hole must be left open.

On Squeaks

All beginners make queer little noises on the Clarinet somewhat like canary pipings, or sometimes agonizing squeals and worse. These "ornaments" are called technically "SQUEAKS."

Squeaks are caused through one or more of the following causes: 1_ When the pupil does not cover the finger holes well, or accidentally touches such keys as I, J, K or F. (With beginners I often prop some cork underneath those keys, putting them out of commission for the time being.) 2_By the pupil overblowing into the instrument, using one pound of air pressure when one ounce is ample. 3_By pressing the reed too much between lip and teeth. 4_ When a reed is much thinner on one side than the other. 5_When the pad of a key does not cover well the hole and the air escapes therefrom. 6_ By playing on a mouthpiece with a warped lay. However, these are matters for the teacher to correct.

Metronome

No musician should be without a metronome. The constant use of this mechanical instrument in technical exercises gives the player a solid sense of rhythm _ an accomplishment many musicians lack. The first Studies in this book should not be played faster than at the rate of 72 quarter notes (or beats) to the minute. ♩ = 72.

How to Practice

1. Never study longer than one hour at a time. Rest at least fifteen minutes and concentrate your mind on any other subject but music, before resuming your playing. No results are possible unless one hour at least a day is given to your instrument.

Divide the hour as follows: 1_ 10 Minutes to scales. 2_ 10 Minutes to sustained tones, including crescendi and diminuendi. 3_ 20 Minutes to technical exercises, including staccato exercises. 4_ 20 Minutes to phrasing lessons.

2. Mark the passages that seem difficult and review them until they are easy to play.

3. Never think of any passage being "hard," (that is within reason); say you are unfamiliar with it and needs more practice.

TABLE of FINGERINGS
for the BOEHM CLARINET
With many Examples illustrating their Practical Use
By GUSTAVE LANGENUS.

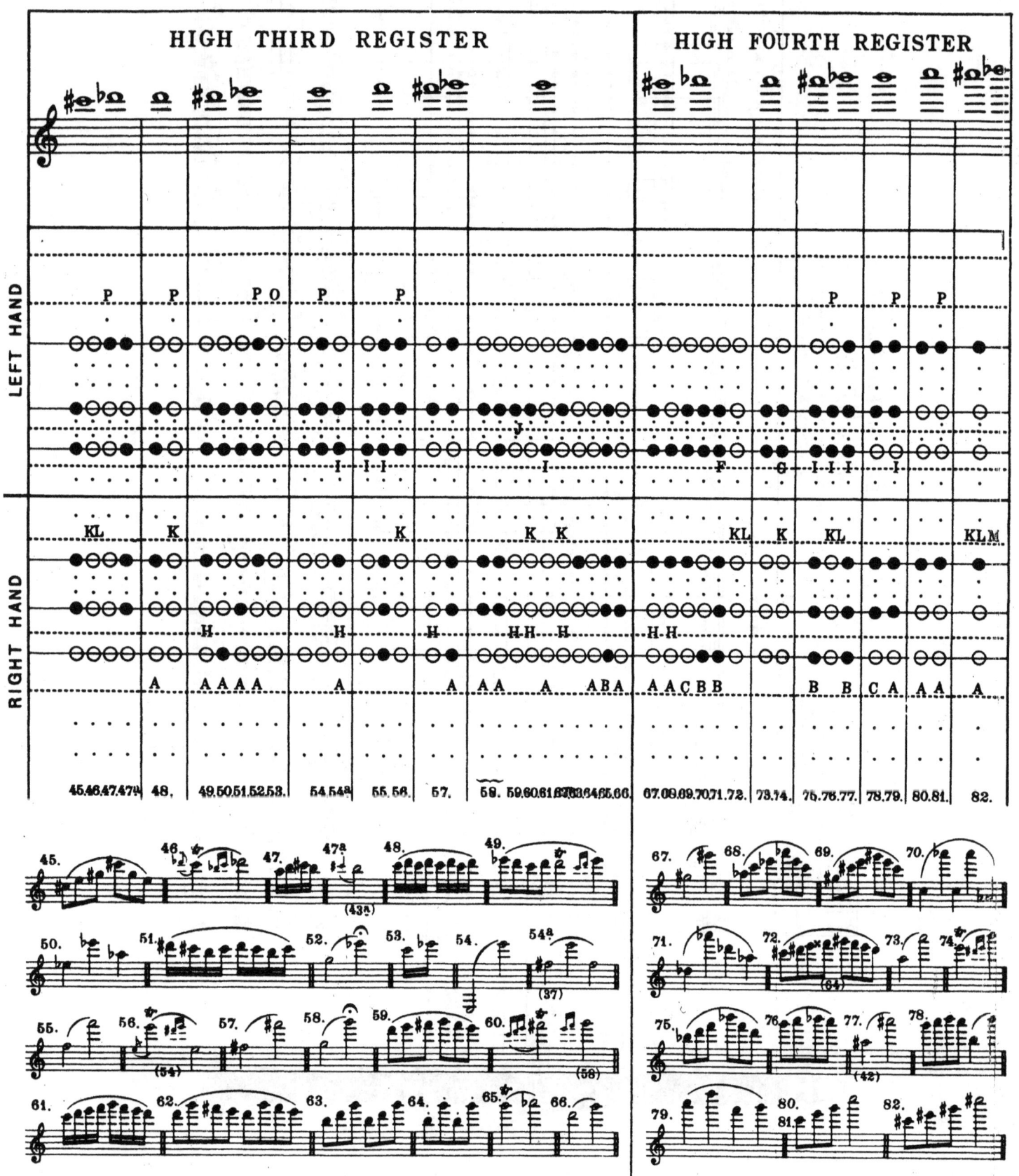

First Book
Preliminary Studies

REMARK 1.— Before starting any of the following exercises, make sure that your embouchure is correctly placed according to your teacher's recommendation or as set forth under the heading of "Embouchure" page VIII.

PRODUCTION OF SOUND. Take a good breath and let the air flow *gently* into the intrument. For the time being all notes must be started by aspirating them, as when saying "hah."

REMARK 2.— The thumb hole remains closed for all the notes, except where an X is marked beneath them, when it must be opened. (There are only five notes for which the thumb must be raised, they are F♯, G, G♯, A and B♭ in the staff.) See also Remark 5, for explanation of the sign ⌒.

Support well the instrument by pressing it upward with the right hand thumb, aided by the thumb-rest.

(1) These trills must be made slowly at first; see Ex. below.
(2) Do not use key P, for this trill, for the time being, play G open.

REMARK 3.— Play all trills thus:

Sustained Tones

REMARK 4.— Always keep the tone well sustained, in other words, let the air enter the instrument as evenly as possible. A tone that shakes or vibrates like a wavering line ~~~~~ is very bad. The curved line ⌒ marked over two or more notes, but of the same name (called a unison), is termed a TIE and means that the last note must not be separated by an articulation from its previous note.

REMARK 5.— When the sign ⌒ is marked above a number of notes it is called a SLUR or LEGATO. This means that the current of air must not be interrupted and the playing be done in a smooth and connected manner. Sustain well the following groups of five notes as if playing only one note. The like of the following are not technical exercises and must not be hurried; they are tone builders and should not be played faster than 72 = ♩

REMARK 6.— Practice the following first without blowing and watch your fingers (see page VII). Get the habit of using key B when playing the low E, when F precedes or follows E.

(See footnote on trills page 1)

Studies on Intervals of a Third

REMARK 7. — The raising or dropping of two or more fingers upon the tone holes or keys must be done exactly like one finger, otherwise an intermediate note will be heard. Practice first without blowing and watch your fingers; no pointed finger joints, fingers must be slightly curved. Study each group in lesson 11 in the following manner:

Ex. A   A few notes more or less do not matter here.

11   A   B   C   D   E   F   G   H   I

Reverse the above exercises by starting with the second note.
The apostrophe "'" means that breath must be taken there.

REMARK 8. — Repeat each bar a number of times. Play them slowly at first and gradually quicken the time. Make a mark of the repeats that seem hard and review them later until the difficulty has disappeared. This should be done with all difficult passages throughout this work.

Studies in the Clarion Register

REMARK 9. — Exercise 17 will help the pupil to get used to the manipulation of **key Q**, commonly called the REGISTER or TWELFTH KEY, the latter being the more correct name. Key Q remains open for all notes from the B (on third line) and upwards.

DO NOT SLIDE THE THUMB TO KEY Q, MANIPULATE IT BY RAISING THE FIRST JOINT OF THE THUMB.

REMARK 10. — If the notes in the clarion-register do not come out well, play study 16, and without changing the embouchure, resume the study in the clarion-register.

SEE REMARK 7, and play the following in the same manner
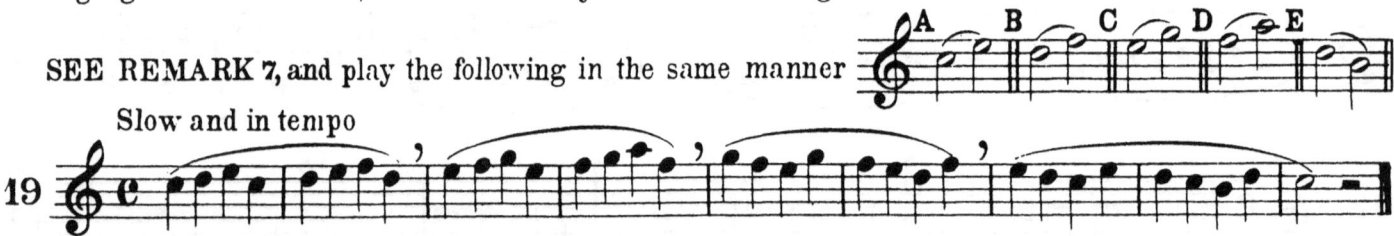

REMARK 11. — The striving for a beautiful tone must alway receive first consideration, phrasing comes next and technic last.

REMARK 12. — Never begin to play without drawing the saliva from the reed and the lay in order to get the emission of a clear tone.

Studies between the Chalumeau and Clarion Registers

The word Chalumeau is the name of an old French instrument, now obsolete, which was the prototype of the Clarinet. Its compass was from the low F to the B♭ on the third line. The name Chalumeau has remained with us to denote the lower compass of the Clarinet from the low E to the B♭. The notes lying between B and C belong to the clarion-register so called on the attributed similarity of tone between these notes on the Clarinet and the tone of the Clarion (a former type of trumpet)

The passage from the chalumeau to the clarion is of great difficulty to beginners. This is because the upper notes of the chalumeau are taken with only one or two fingers while the lower notes of the clarion require not less than eight or nine fingers, and these must fall upon the holes and keys strictly together, otherwise a disagreeable squeak ensues.

As a preparatory for bridging the two registers a few exercises are first given (23, 24)

REMARK 13.— Do not finger the A with the tip of the finger to avoid sliding to the tone hole; always make the A by tilting the hand upward so that the key is touched with the SIDE of the index.

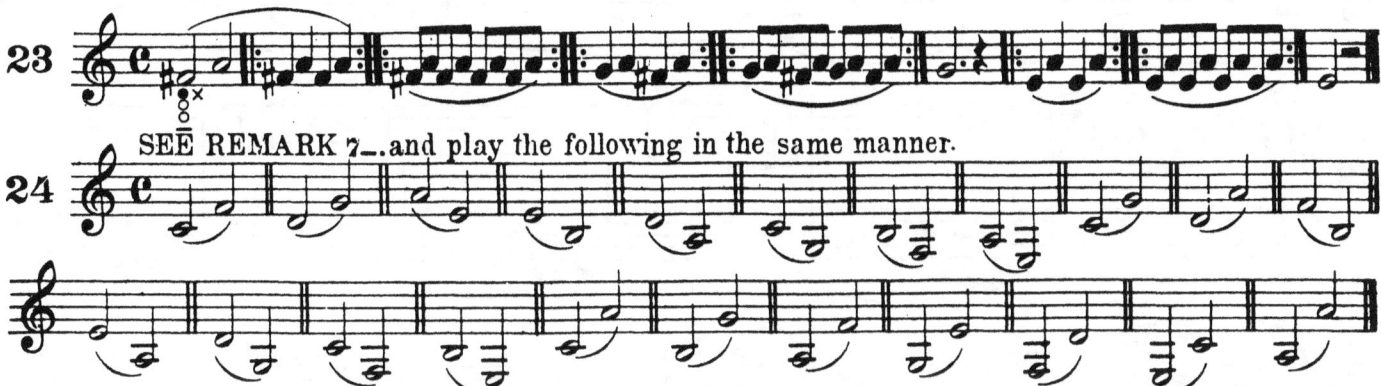

REMARK 14.— Whenever possible, let the right hand fingers rest upon the holes especially when playing from any of the following notes to this greatly facilitates the passage from the chalumeau to the clarion.

To denote when the right hand fingers have to remain upon the holes, the following signs are used in this Method.

⌊O⎯⎯⎯⎯⌋ Denotes: Keep fingers on one or more holes.
⌊E⎯⎯⎯⎯⌋ Denotes: Keep finger upon key E.
⌊Eo⎯⎯⎯⌋ Denotes: Keep fingers upon key E and holes.

REMARK 15.— Do not force the notes of the clarion-register. Too much pressure between teeth and lip is bad; press corners of lips chiefly, and inwardly.

Rhythmic Studies in 2/4, 3/4 and 4/4 time

REMARK 16.— In the following duets the first part does not contain any technical difficulties, however, the notes must be played very slowly with all the attention centred on the production of a beautiful tone and great eveness of execution. The second part should be studied when more advanced.

KLOSÉ

BERR

Staccato Studies

REMARK 17.— Read carefully what has been written in the introduction regarding the action of the tongue. In the next study the notes must be sounded with emphasis, but without any exaggeration.

Keep the reed free as much as possible from saliva in order to have the tone clear.

REMARK 18.— In the following two studies the action of the tongue must be exceedingly light; the least possible effort made, the better the result. Make sure that both eighth notes are evenly short.

41

42

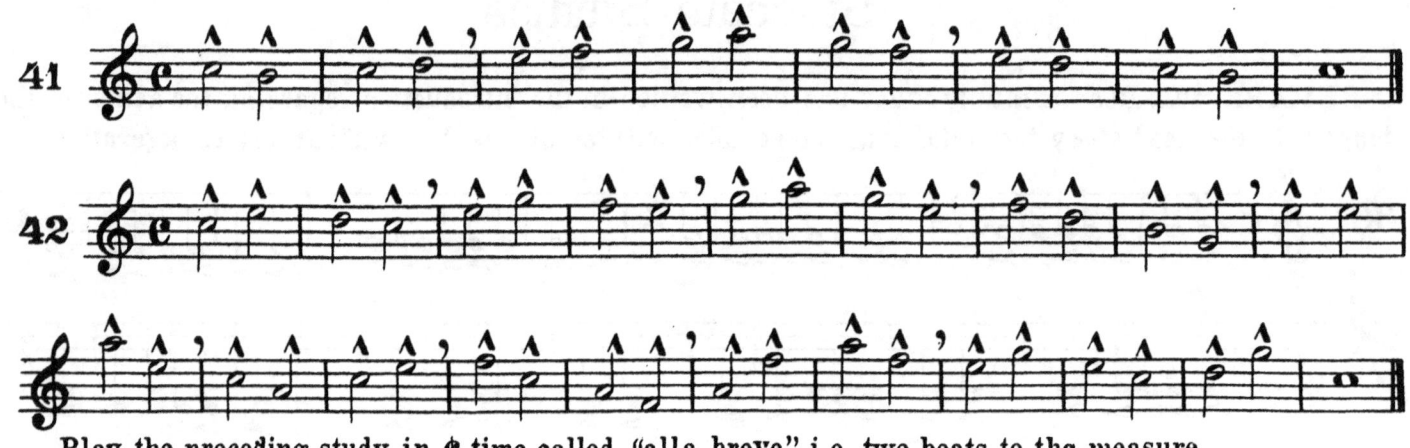

Play the preceding study in ¢ time called "alla breve," i.e. two beats to the measure.

43

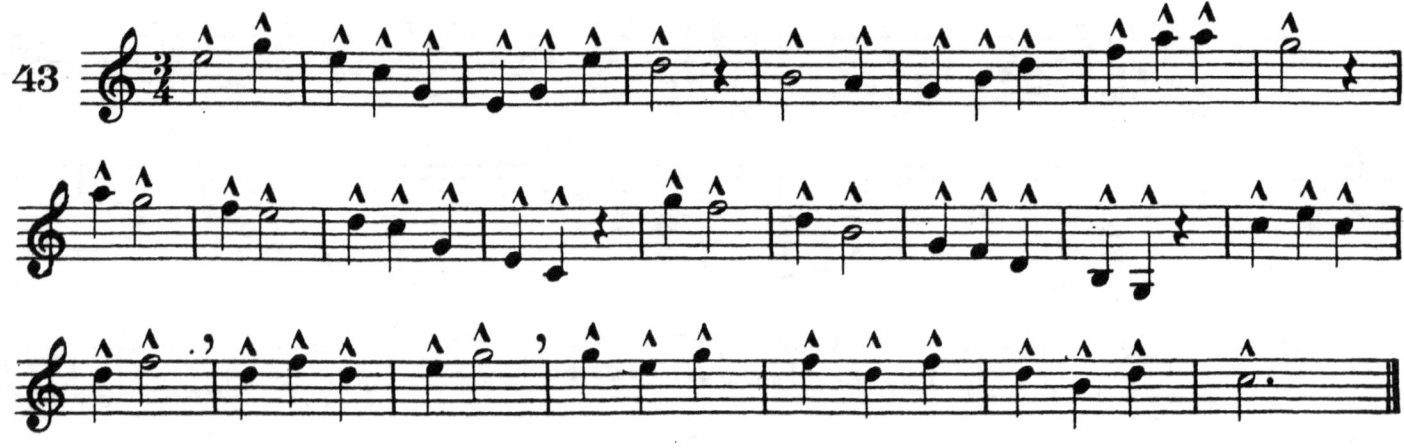

Subdivide the notes in studies **37, 41,** and **43** into sixteenth notes and play them softly.

SEE REMARK 18

44

45

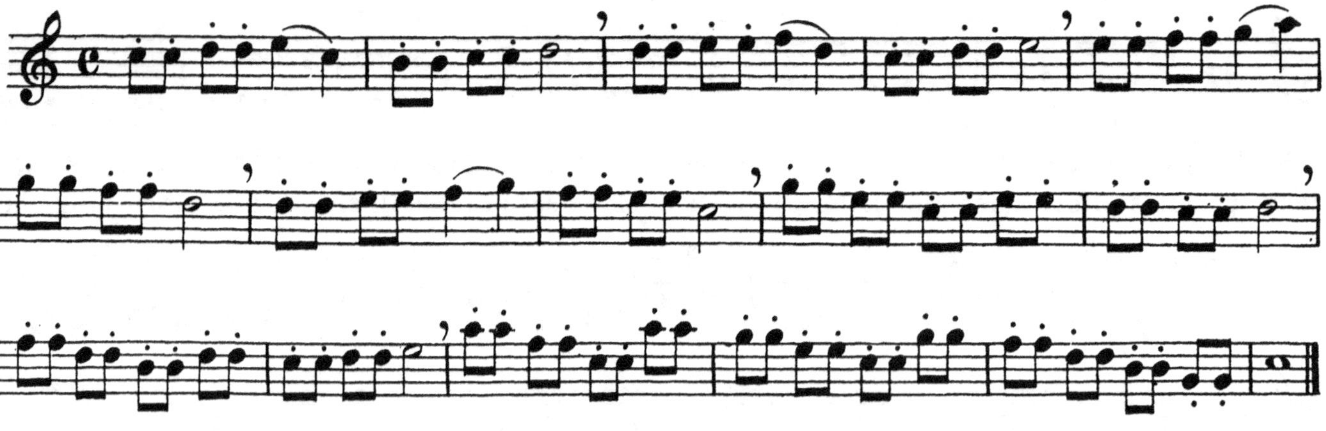

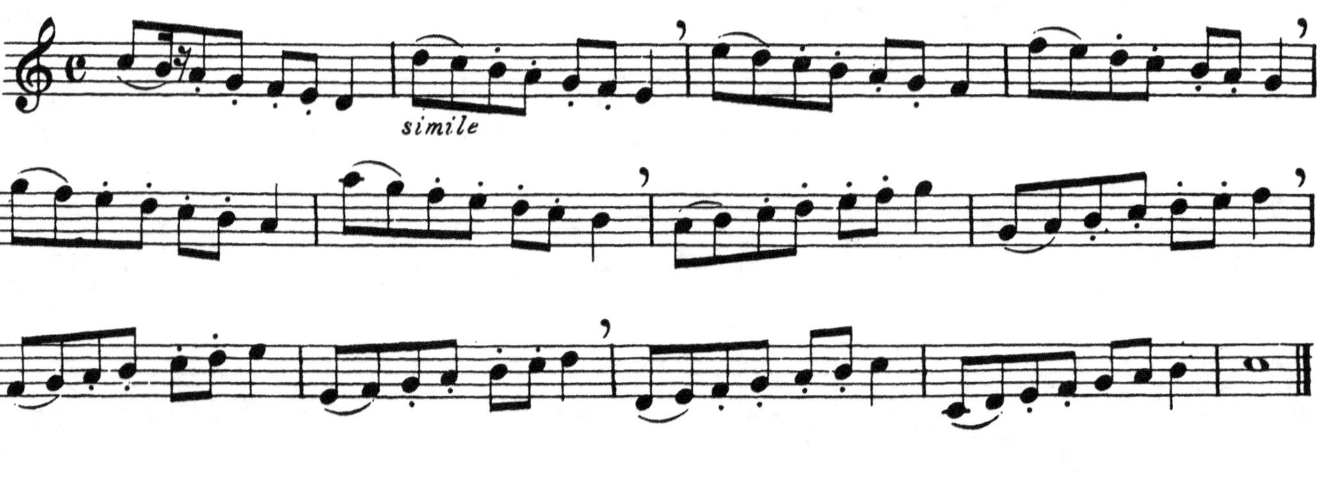

Studies for the High B and C

REMARK 20.— To get the higher notes, contract the throat a little more than for the lower notes, using also a slightly lower lip pressure upon the reed, this is accomplished by bringing the jaw slightly forward.

Repeat each measure 4 times.

50.

SEE REMARK 7.— Practice the following study in the same manner.

51.

C major scale. To be memorized.

52.

53.

54.

(1) The dash "—" over a note means that the note must be gently articulated and **fully sustained**.

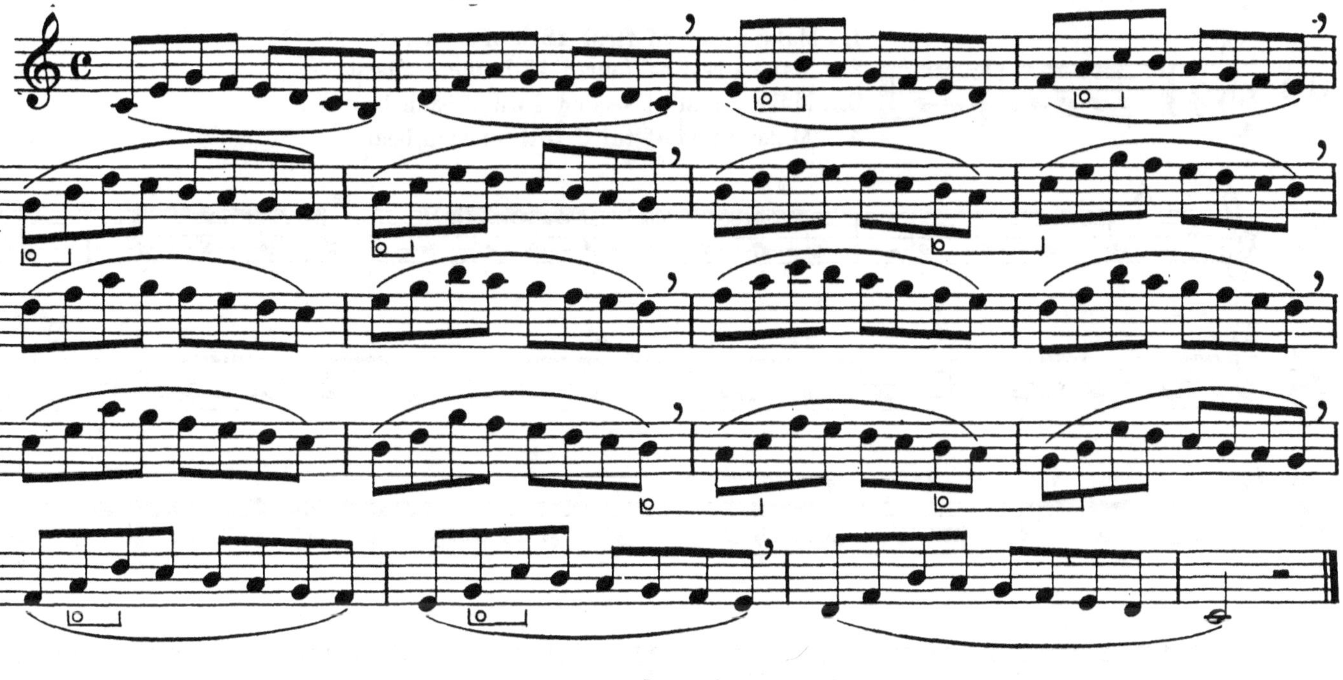

Articulation

Articulation in music refers to the art of linking musical sounds by various forms of legato and staccato. The student should carefully study the preceding exercise with the different articulations as shown in the following examples. Always play the legato notes a little louder than the staccato, in order to give greater lightness to the latter.

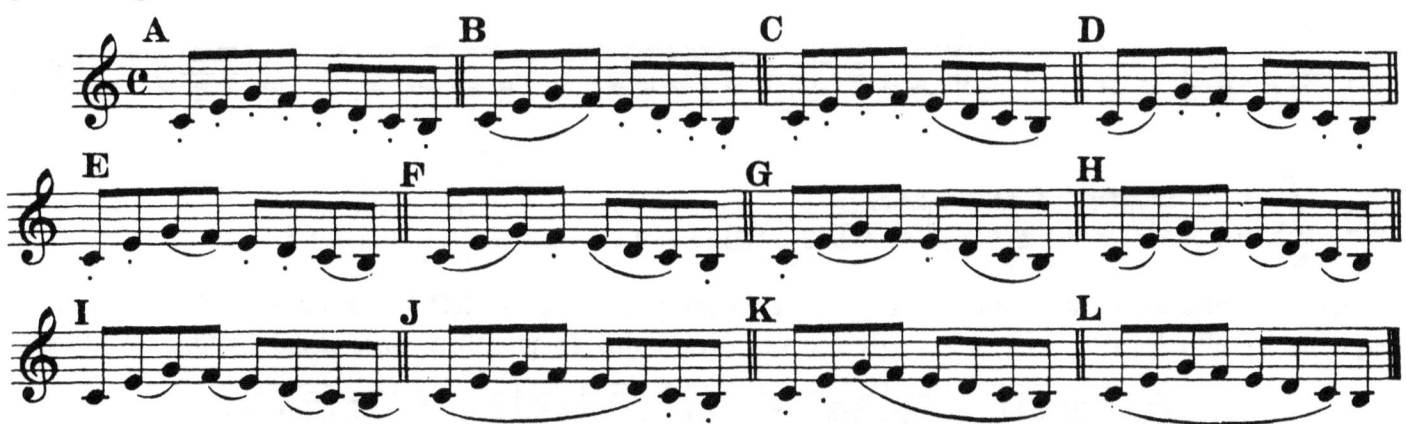

Rhythmic Studies

Some pupils have a weak sense of rhythm; to strengthen this the following exercises are given. The teacher need not give this whole page for his pupil to practice, but can select those rhythms that are appropriate for the time being. The following exercises must be done with different notes, preferably in scale form(1). USE METRONOME.

57 
- 1st time;—substitute 8th rest for the 1st eighth note. (1)
- 2nd „   „   „   „   „   2nd   „   „
- 3rd „   „   „   „   „   3rd   „   „
- 4th „   „   „   „   „   4th   „   „
- 5th „   „   „ rests „ „ 1st & 4th „ notes
- 6th „   „   „   „   „   2nd & 3rd „   „

58 
- Make a rest alternately of each 8th note.
- Make a rest alternately of each two 8th notes.

59 
- 1—. Make a rest alternately of each 8th note.
- 2—. Make a rest of the first and fourth 8th notes.
- 3—. Make a rest of the second and fifth 8th notes.

60 
- 1—. Make a rest of first 16th of each beat.
- 2—. Make a rest of fourth 16th of each beat.
- 3—. Make a rest of second 16th of each beat.
- 4—. Make a rest of third 16th of each beat.

61 A

B

C

D

E   F

G

32 
- 1—. Make a rest alternately of each 16th note.
- 2—. Make a rest alternately of two 16th notes.

The different combinations in this example are inexhaustable and are left to the teacher's discretion. The pupil, even well advanced, will necessarily have to review this frequently as some of the rhythms are difficult.

(1)

Second Book
Studies for the F♯ Fingerings

REMARK 21. — There are two fingerings for this F♯. In these exercises the F♯ must be taken with the index finger of the left hand. Be careful not to raise the other fingers too high when playing the F♯. If necessary the little finger can close key E, thus insuring the correct position of the left hand.

REMARK 22. — This F♯ must be fingered thus:

REMARK 23. — Take the low F♯ in these exercises with key C.

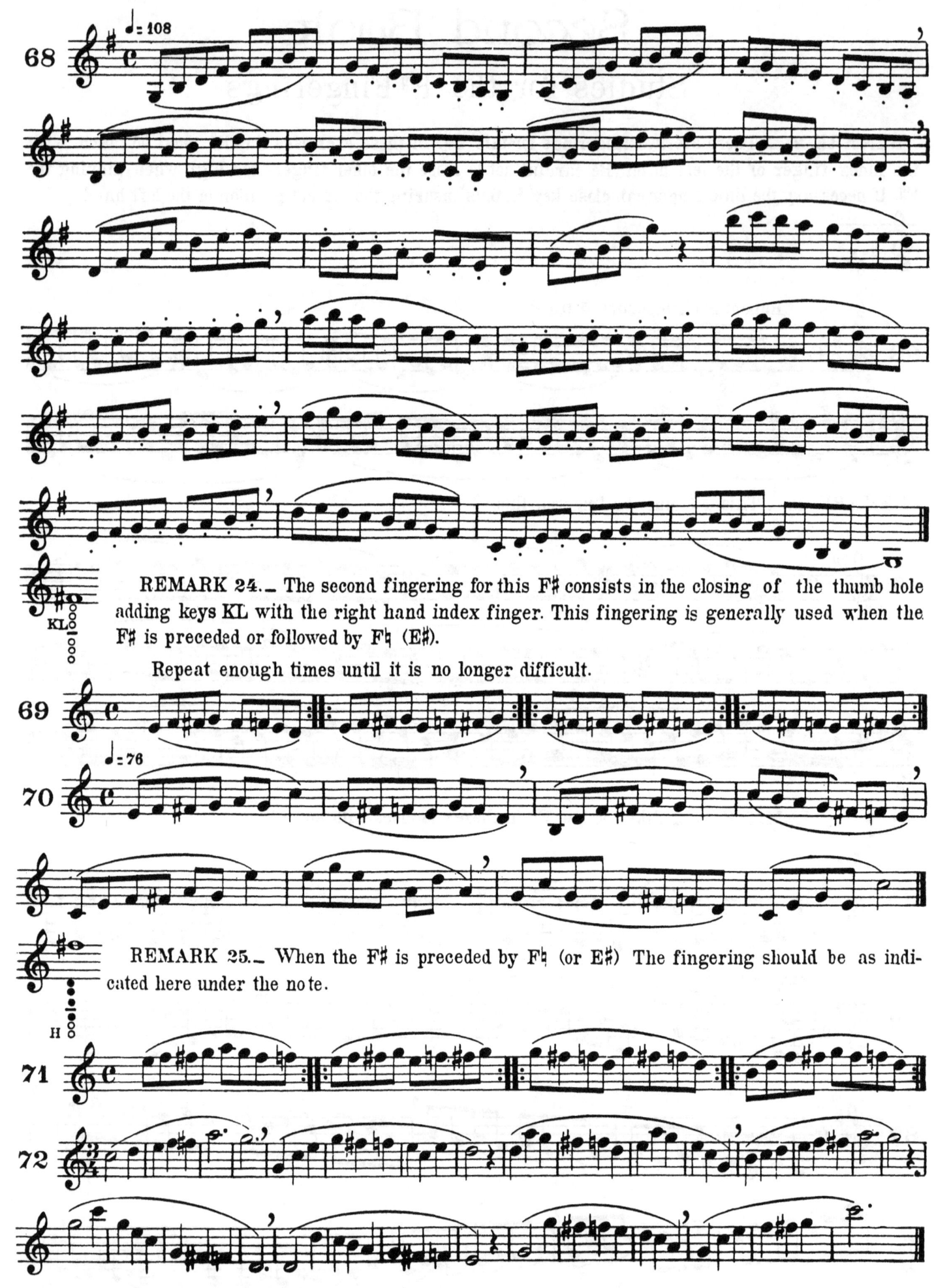

SEE REMARK 7 And practice studies, 11, 24, 46 and 51, substituting F♯ for F♮.

Rhythmic Studies

Studies **79** and **80** are often played with the sixteenth notes sounding like thirty seconds or more often like eighth notes in $\frac{12}{8}$ time. The dotted eighth notes being usually held not long enough. The following studies will probably help to give the exact feeling of the value of the sixteenth.

Practise the last study with variations of rhythm as in study 76, A, B, C and D.

Studies on Dotted Notes

Sustain the dotted eighth notes to the fullest extent.

BERR

Play also 79 and 80 with dotted 8th notes subdivided into three 16th notes.

BERR

On Rhythm and Syncopation

DEFINITION: Rhythm is the steady recurrence of accented and unaccented sounds. A musician is said to have a good rhythm when he plays in good time neither dragging nor anticipating the tempo.

Syncopation is formed when a note begins on an unaccented part of a measure and is sustained over the accented part.

Some students find great difficulty in learning to play syncopated music, the cause of this is that they probably have been badly taught or lack a sense of rhythm. It is thus necessary for them to cultivate a good rhythm before studying syncopation. To acquire this, I generally recommend the pupil to beat time to the beats of a Metronome; if he has none, I then advise him to listen carefully to regularly recurring noises, such as the tick-tack of a clock, the trotting of a horse, or the marching of soldiers, whilst beating time energetically to these divers noises. At first it takes great concentration to beat time correctly, but soon one does it instinctively.

By listening carefully, it will be noted that one noise is slightly louder than the other, and if we beat time to them we will, by instinct, beat One (down beat) for the louder noise, and Two (up beat) for the weaker noise. Musically speaking, the first is the accented, and the second the unaccented beat. If a note occurs on an unaccented beat and ends on, or includes, an accented beat, it becomes then a syncopated note.

In the next study the syncopation comes on the second beat and is tied over the accented beat of the following measure.

In 4/4 time the first and third are accented beats, the second and fourth are unaccented.

The next study shows the syncopation on the second beat tied over to the accented third beat. In study 83 syncopation comes on the second and fourth beats.

REMARK 26 — Sustain well the notes.

In 3/4 time there is only one accented beat, the second and third being unaccented beats.

In study 84 the syncopation occurs on the second beat, and in the following study it comes on the third beat.

REMARK 27.— (1) When taking breath in the middle of a passage, do it quickly through the mouth; in cases like this, play the A as if an 8th note, followed by an 8th rest. The principal object being to come on time with the note following the breathing.

If a quarter note is subdivided into two eighth notes, then we have the same characteristics of the $\frac{2}{4}$ time, inasmuch as the first eighth is accented and the second unaccented. Hence the same rule applies to syncopation for eighths as for quarter notes. See page 20.

For convenience of writing, composers would write the above study in the following manner.

REMARK 28.— The note preceding or following a syncopation should always be cut shorter than its value. The first bar in the next study is an example how to play the rest.

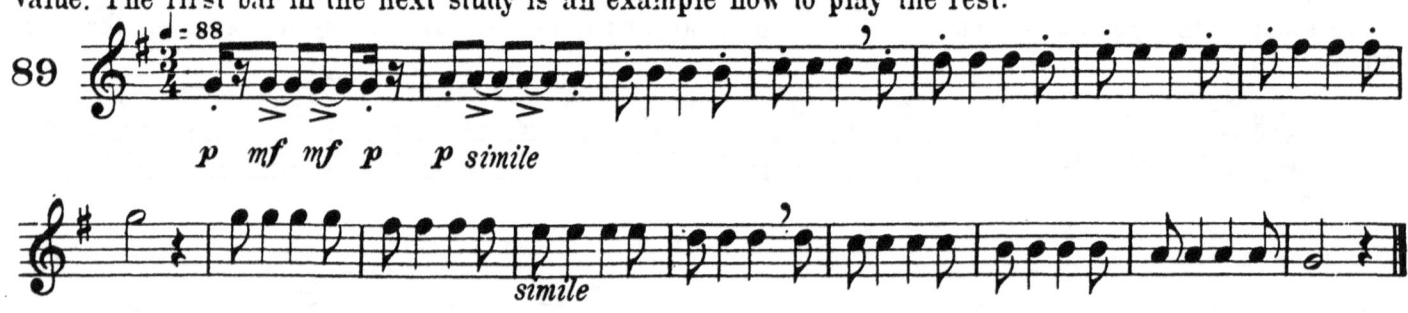

REMARK 29.— Syncopated notes are always accented; the eighth notes preceding or following must not only be played short, but also soft and light.

(1) To be studied also thus:

Studies for the High D

REMARK 30. — This D has a very harsh sound; care must be taken to make it sound nice. To get the high notes, use a slightly lower pressure on the reed by bringing the jaw a little more forward.

Technical Studies

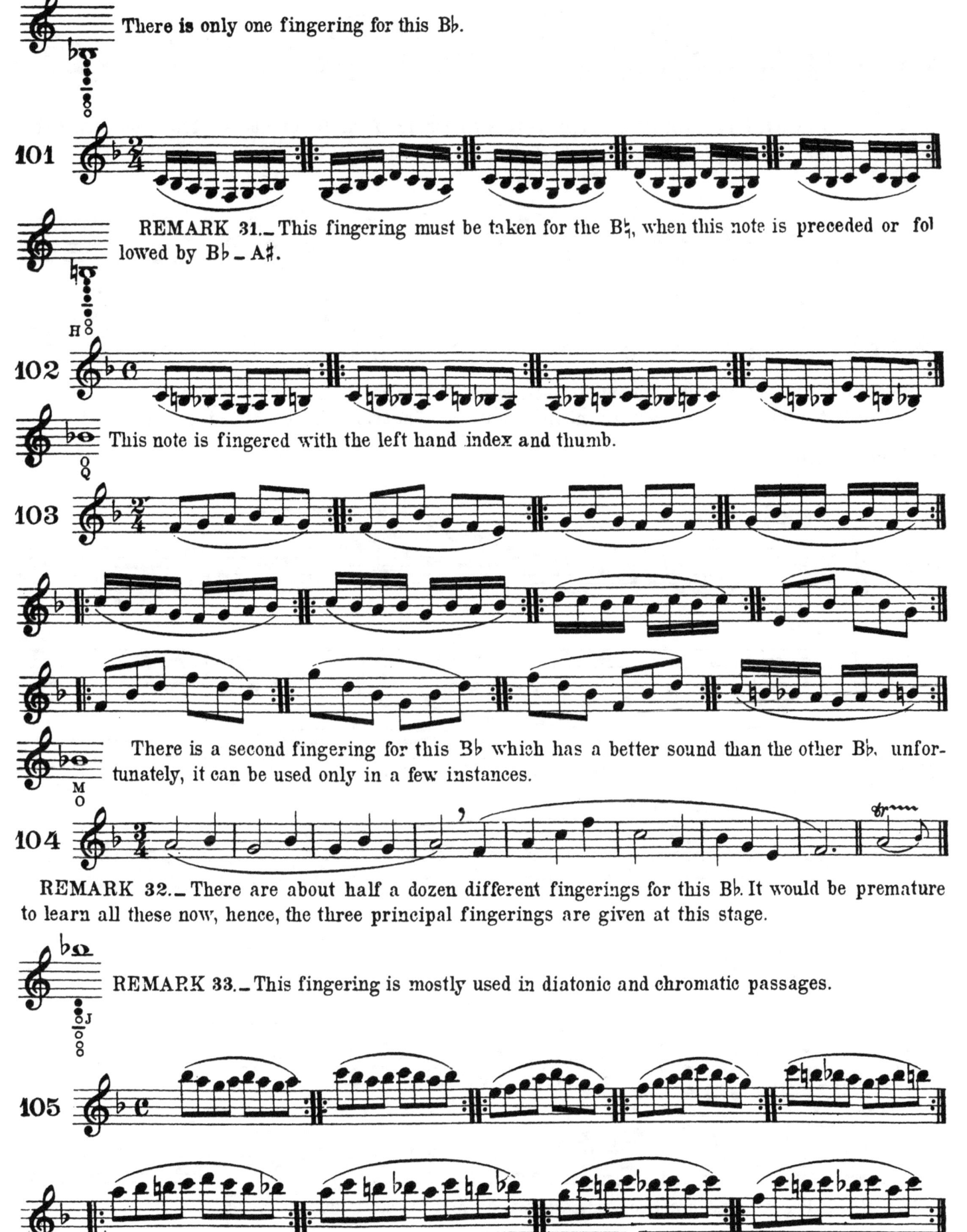

28

REMARK 34. — To be fingered in this manner when the G, A♭ or G♯ precedes or follows the B♭.

106

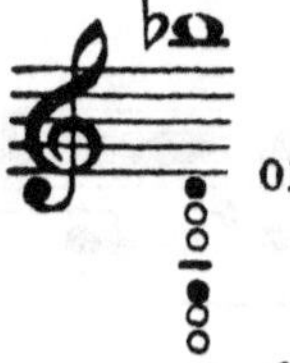

REMARK 35. — On most Clarinets this fingering of the B♭ produces a better tone, than either of the aforementioned B♭ fingerings. It must be used in all the instances as follow.

107

REMARK 36. — I advise the student to pencil every B♭ fingering that occurs in the next F major studies, according to the three rules as just given. Abbreviate the fingerings in the following manner: letter J for J, K for K, and 1 for

F Major Scale

108

109

SEE REMARK 7. — And practice studies 11, 24, 46, and 51 substituting B♭ for B♮.

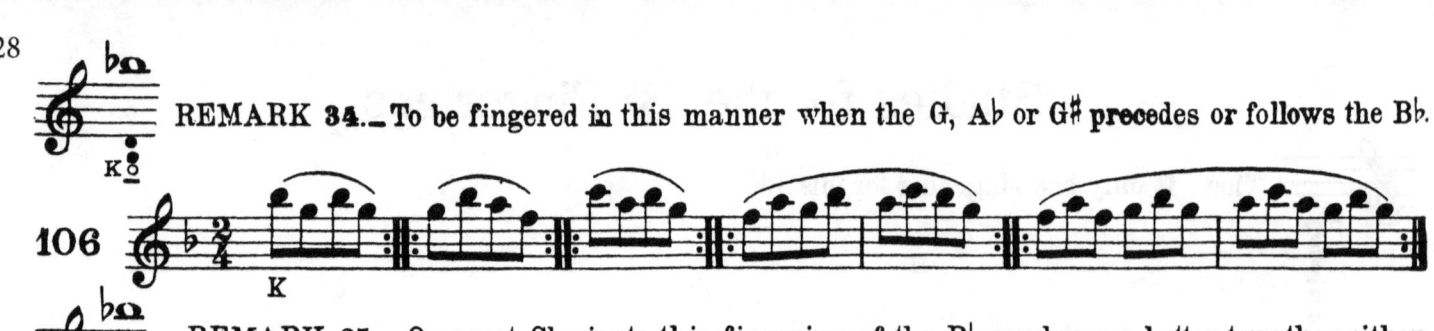

Rhythmic Studies in 6/8 time

REMARK 37.— When sixteenth notes occur in 6/8 time, care must be taken that the sixteenths come exactly on their respective time value, especially when a sixteenth follows a dotted eighth note like in Variation II. This is often played like a thirty-second note by careless musicians. In order to perform this correctly, the player must be conscious of the subdivision of each eighth note into two sixteenths. The following will make this clear.

Third Book

Studies for the C♯-D♭ Fingerings
Special Remarks on Keys E-D and C-F

Forte and Piano

These two Italian words *Forte* and *Piano* mean respectively loud and soft. Abbreviated by f forte and p for piano they are placed under the notes to indicate what intensity of sound must be given to the music. Forte and Piano are to the musician what light and shade are to the painter; both artists must know how to use these effects skillfully in order to instill life into their work.

In order to obtain a distinct contrast between the forte and the piano in the next study, the student must sustain the forte with a full level tone for seven beats without increasing or diminishing the sound. In the same manner the following note in piano must sound like an echo of the previous note. In short, control well the breath, and let the air flow freely into the instrument producing a beautifully even tone devoid of any shakiness.

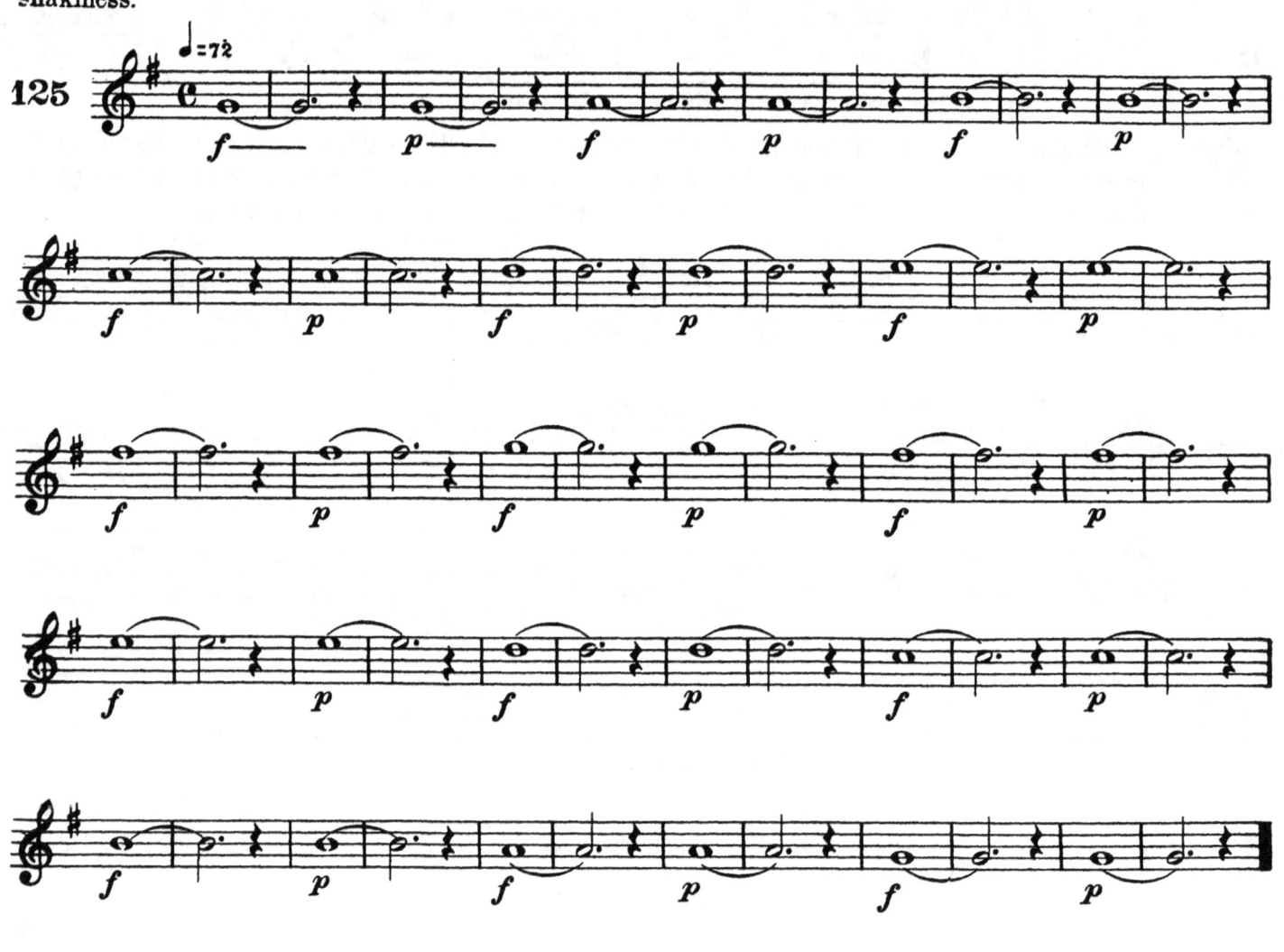

Crescendo and Diminuendo

Crescendo means increasing, i. e. in loudness. Decrescendo (or diminuendo) means decreasing. Both words are often contracted as *cresc.* and *decresc.* They are also expressed by ⟨=== for crescendo and ===⟩ for decrescendo.

To make an effective crescendo the tone must swell gradually and nobly as the sign indicates ⟨=== not by steps or wobbly like this ~~~~~~~ or ⟨

It is of the greatest importance to notice how far a crescendo extends to the *forte* or other nuance it may lead to; sometimes it must be made in one beat and often it extends over a number of bars. In any case the volume and increase of tone must be regulated according to the length of the crescendo. The reverse applies to the decrescendo.

REMARK 43ª.– Be careful the tone does not become coarse by the time the forte is reached.

126

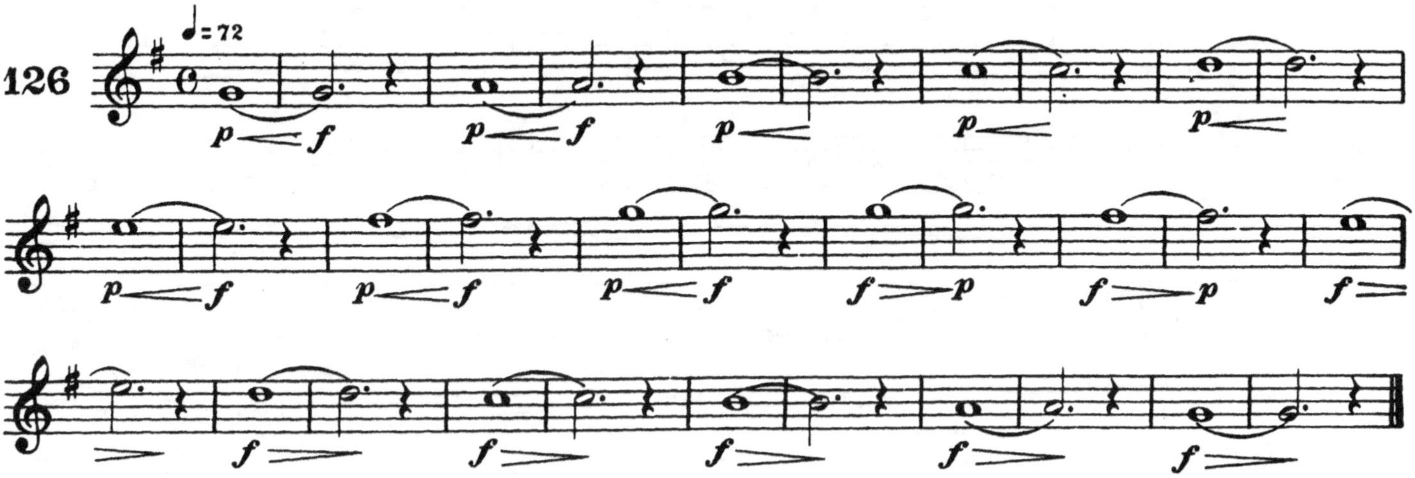

127

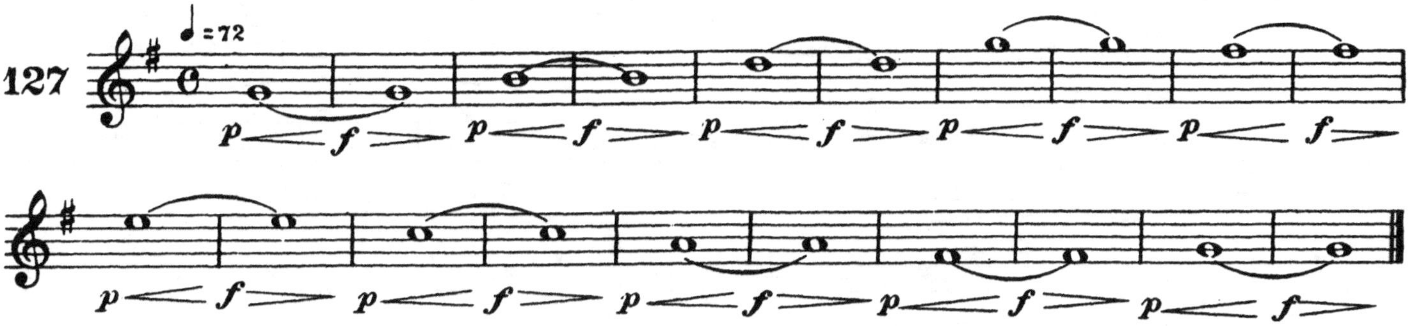

REMARK 44.– In the next passage the crescendo and decrescendo must be made as if playing only one note while the fingers raise or fall without perturbing the sound gradation.

128

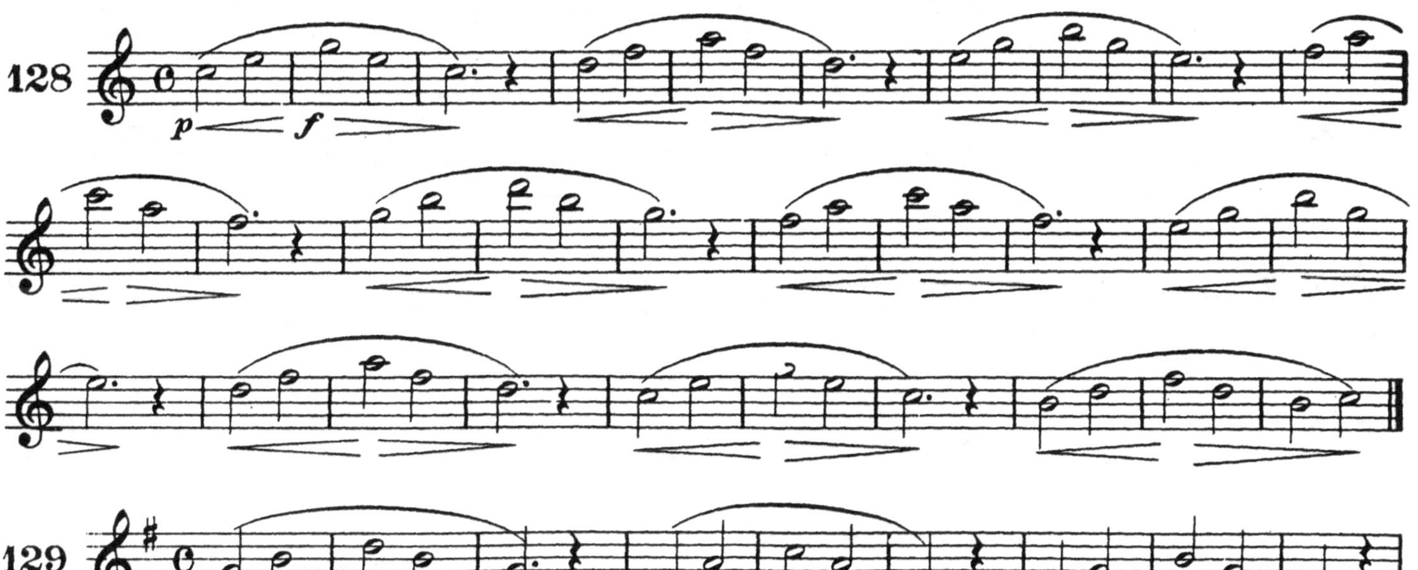

129

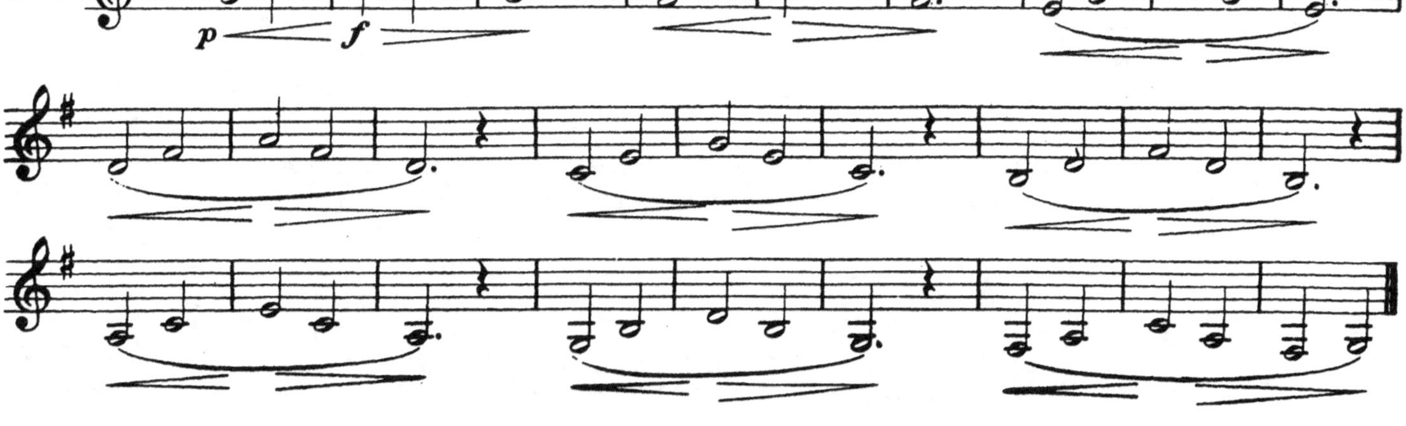

Theme and Variations

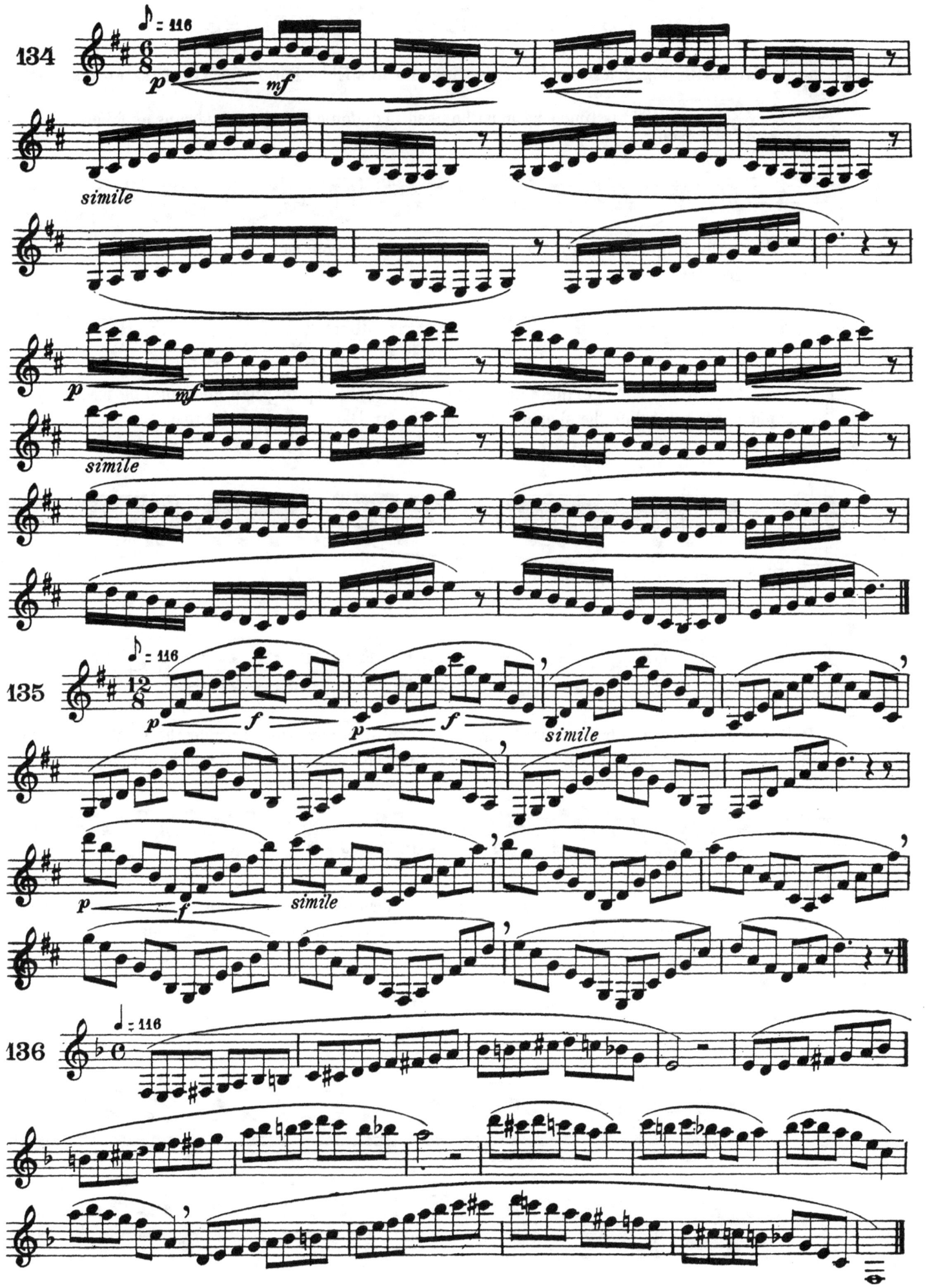

Romance

Play these exercises as evenly as possible. Pencil the bars that are "hard" **and go back to them** until the difficulty has disappeared.

Fourth Book
Studies for the G♯-A♭ Fingerings

There is only one fingering for this G♯.

REMARK 51.— Mention has already been made in Remark 47 page 40 about key G. This fingering must also be used for the low F when the G♯ precedes or follows F.

The above Remark applies to the C when it precedes or follows the D♯.

There is only one fingering for this G♯. It is taken with the left hand index.

REMARK 52.— There are two fingerings for this G♯. The first one is chiefly used.

REMARK 53.— The second fingering has a dull unreliable tone, and is used only in quick passages to avoid the awkward gliding the first fingering would necessitate in the following passages.

REMARK 54.— On page 27, Remark 32, it was mentioned that there are six different fingerings for this B♭. The three most important ones were explained. The others are only possible in quick passages. Fingering 4 is used in going from F♯ to A♯ (see Ex. I); however it makes the B♭ much too sharp, as does 5, and must never be used in slow passages. Fingering 6 is mainly used for trilling A♭-B♭; I use a forked B♭ on my instrument, and it gives satisfaction in such passages as at Ex. II, and III.

REMARK 55.— On page 32, Remark 41, I pointed out that it is sometimes compulsory to use key D instead of key E; this is particularly necessary when the intervening note between the low E and G♯ is either C♮ or F♯.

REMARK 56.— Key D must be used for the B♮ when the intervening note between B and D♯ (E♭) is either C♮ or C♯ (D♭.)

SEE REMARK 7. And practice studies 11, 24, 46 and 51, substituting B♭-E♭-A♭, for B♮-E♮-A♮. Also F♯-C♯-G♯-D♯-A♯, for F♮-C♮-G♮-D♮-A♮.

Studies in Crescendi and Diminuendi

The following studies are intended to make the embouchure and tone flexible.

Marks of Expression

Reference has already been made on page **34** regarding the *forte* and *piano*. Each of these has closely allied shadings as is seen in the following table:

Nuances	Marked	Meaning	Effect
Pianissimo	*pp*	very soft	Mysteriousness. Echo
Piano	*p*	soft	Image of night. Tranquility.
Mezzo piano	*mp*	slightly louder than *p*	
Mezzo forte	*mf*	half loud	Image of day. Joyful
Forte	*f*	loud	
Fortissimo	*ff*	very loud	Strength. Dignity. Massiveness

The observance of these nuances, as marked in music, must be strictly adhered to, in order to make the performance vivid and interesting.

Studies in Dynamics
Sound Gradations

REMARK 57. — Be exceedingly careful in attacking the notes in the next exercise. Let the action of the tongue be as light as possible when attacking notes in *pp*, and more pronounced for the louder nuances. Do not make any crescendi or diminuendi but sustain well every shading. When playing *ff* aim at seccuring as beautiful a tone as in *mf*. Do not imitate the musician who misinterprets *ff* as a sign for playing with a coarse and blatant tone.

This is an important practice, and should often be played with other notes.

On Expression

At this stage it is assumed that the student has a fair control of the embouchure, and has acquired a certain amount of technic. Being free, to some extent, from these material difficulties, the mind is in a receptive state for greater improvement.

Now comes one of the most important steps to be taken in the course of musical education. This consists of acquiring an insight into the meaning of compositions, and the interpretation of the same.

Every musical work expresses something; sorrow, merriment, melancholy, sprightliness, terror, peacefulness, passion, etc., and each composition has its tone gradations, slight and quick hurryings, tarryings, pauses, agitations, and different tone coloring. It is not always possible to denote these different shadings with signs in the music, and it is often left to the performer to feel these things and give life to them. These nuances, and the best manner of interpreting the composer's intentions, together with adding one's own individuality to it, is summed up in *Expressive playing*.

As the necessary equipment for learning the greatest art of instrumental music, i.e. musical or expressive interpretation, the clarinetist should have:

First, a beautiful tone; second, an even technic; third, a flexible embouchure, that is, be able to make evenly, short and long crescendi from *p* to *f*, and decrescendi from *f* to *p*; fourth, a clear attack of notes at any shading; and fifth, a good control of the breath.

Having the above necessary qualifications - and they are all acquirable - there are three important **matters** to be considered when playing cantabile music, viz:

1. Give as much attention to one note as to the next, none must slip by, everyone is important.

2. Observe carefully the expression marks, especially in works of standard composers, and instill life into them. In so-called "popular music" the nuances are often left out entirely, or badly marked, and the performer needs good schooling to supply the deficiencies. Infinite pains have been taken in marking the nuances in this method. Study them well. Note particularly whether a phrase begins *piano* or *mezzoforte*, and whether it leads to a *mf* or a *f*. As an exercise, copy a lesson out of this book, without the expression or legato marks. Close the book, and an hour or two afterwards, mark the slurs, expression and breathing marks, etc; and compare the copy with the book.

3. Note whether the melody is in a jolly or a sad mood, and let your own feeling and playing be accordingly. For instance, in Duo No. 177, we note the key is A minor. Music in minor keys is always melancholic. The melody is slow and must be played without haste. The first note is *piano*, and a slight crescendo leads to F, marked *mf*; this F is the principal note of that group of five notes and is therefore brought out stronger than the others. The same applies to the G♯ in the fourth bar. In the fifth bar the swelling of the tone must be more marked than in the previous two cases, inasmuch as this leads to a *forte* on the C; the C is the principal note of the first eight bars, and as such is called the *Climax*; the notes in the previous bars have all been leading towards this C, and the following two bars recede from it. Then follows a restless figure of two bars that can be taken a little faster; the next two bars, almost the same figure, should be played slower, as in the first tempo, these leading to the climax on the D. The next six bars are played similarly to the first six, excepting that the climax is on E, which is deliberately marked *mf* instead of *f*, on account of its shrill sound. The piece is brought to a subdued close by the last two bars.

Duo No. 178, on the contrary, is gay and must be played in a moderately **quick** time and as **sprightly as** possible. Analyze the other duos in the same manner.

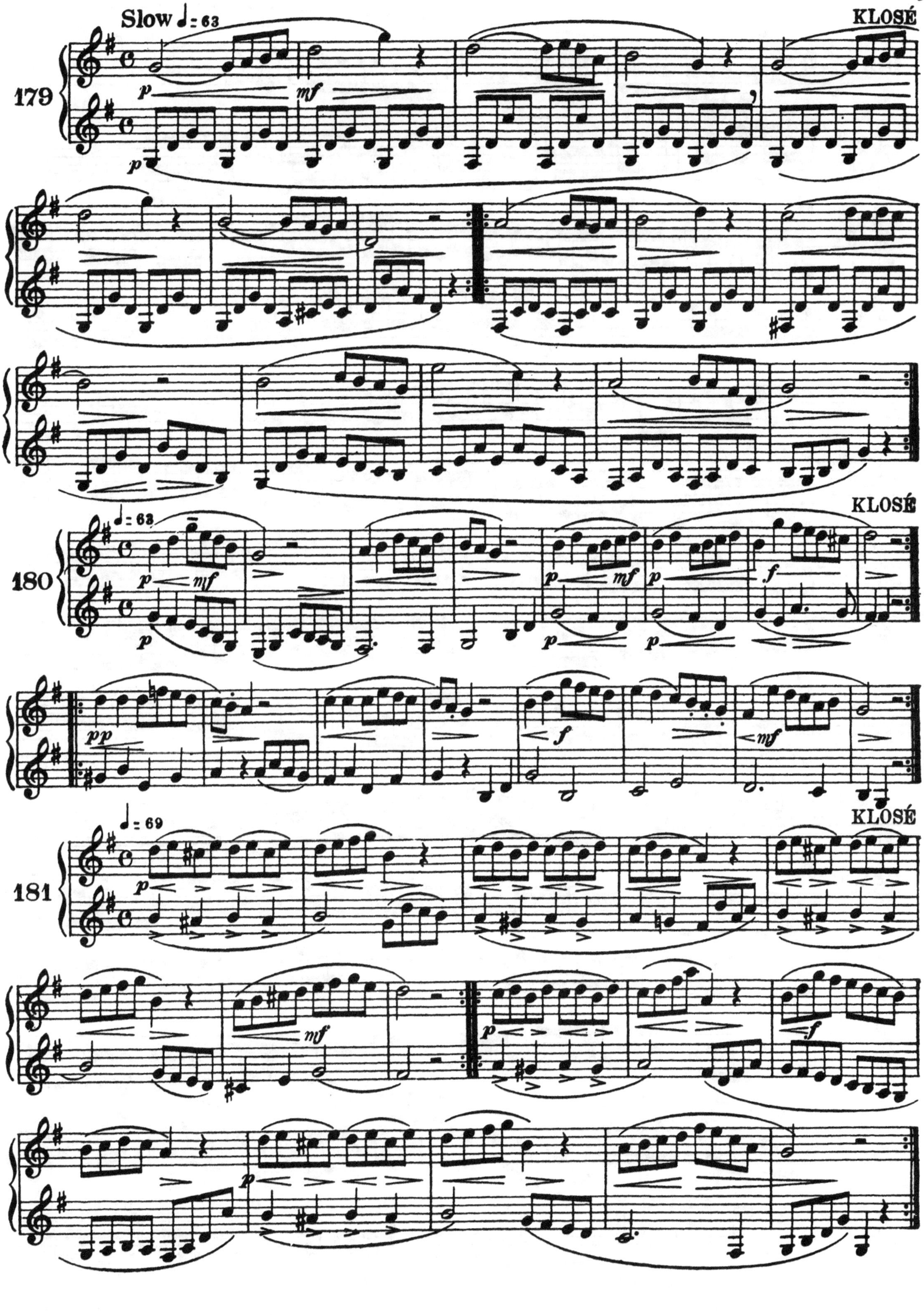
Slow ♩= 63
KLOSÉ
179
♩= 63
KLOSÉ
180
♩= 69
KLOSÉ
181

REMARK.—58 The second Clarinet must always subdue his tone to **the first Clarinet**, except where the second has the melody.

(1) For the meaning of these Italian terms, see page 87 and 88
(2) Dots placed over **notes** in **slow music** means that the notes must be **separated** delicately with a soft stroke of the tongue.

The first eight bars must be played with great simplicity, and the four bars following with great warmth.

(1) A dash (–) over a note means that the note must be hold a little longer than its value.

The sixteenths must be well detached and played with great firmness.

+) A fermata or pause sign: "⌒" lengthens the value of a **note, or rest,** for an indefinite time.

Syncopation Studies

Remember **Remarks** 28 and 29, page 22.

Fifth Book
Distorted Rhythms

REMARK 59.— On page 26 and 29 I have already drawn the student's attention to the subdivision of eighth notes into sixteenths in order to give the correct time value to the latter. The observance of this is very important; in slow tempi it is absolutely necessary to subdivide quarter notes into eighths, and eighth notes into sixteenths. Very seldom do we hear a correct performance of the opening bars of Suppé's Overture "Poet and Peasant," the sixteenth notes being, almost invariably, played like thirty-seconds:

REMARK 60.— This is only one instance out of many similar passages in different works. The student must beware of making such careless mistakes. If players would subdivide the above example as marked at A, such violations of rhythm could not possibly happen.

Rhythm is also often distorted in 6/8 time, the eighth notes being played like sixteenths. This is not only a violation of rhythm, but it changes the character of the music from 6/8 to 2/4 time, which is vastly different.

REMARK 61.— Triplets are often played wrongly, to-wit:

REMARK 62. — In Auber's "Masaniello" Overture, this figure ♪♪♪ ♪♪♪ is often played ♪♪♪ ♪♪♪. To remedy this, play the passage a few times using the first note twice instead of the rest, as in 2nd and 3rd bars. Then play as written, thinking of a note instead of a rest. Practice also study (A) leaving out the first eighth of each beat.

(1) Special care must be taken to play the two eighth notes evenly; very often they are played thus: (♩ ♪♪♪) like a quarter note in 6/8 time.

The Forte Piano (fp)

REMARK 63.— This term indicates that the note marked *fp* must be attacked *forte* and suddenly drop to *piano*.

The Sforzando or Sforzato

REMARK 64. — *sf* - This word means "forced." When placed under a note abbreviated by *sf* it denotes that the note must be attacked with force and emphasis. The *sf* differs from the *fp*, in that the tone does not suddenly drop but makes a slight diminuendo. The attack is also done with a greater wind pressure than is the case in the *fp*.

REMARKS 65. — When a *sf* occurs in a *piano* passage, the notes following the *sf* must return immediately to *piano*. The same applies when it occurs in *pp* or *f* passages. I mention this because many musicians think that *sf* means forte for the rest of a passage.

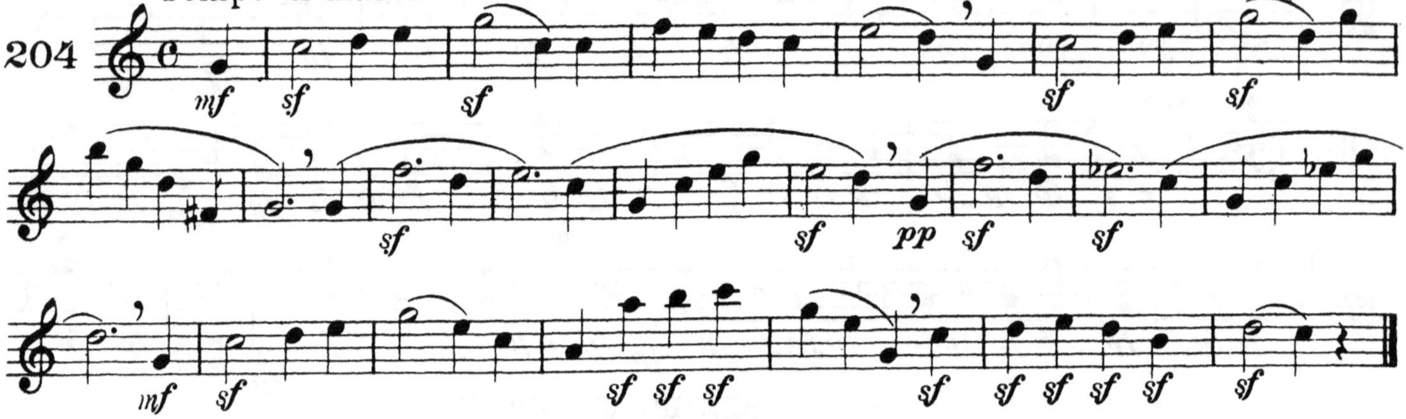

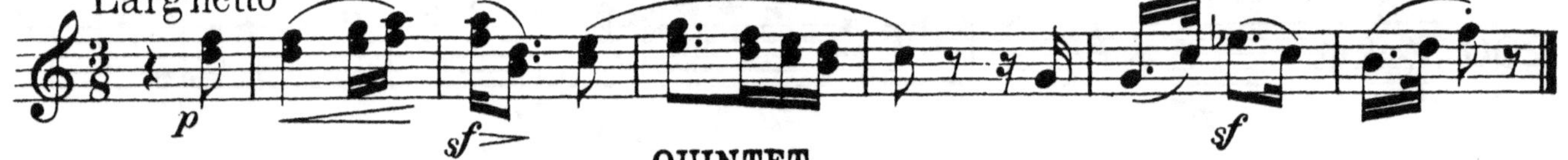

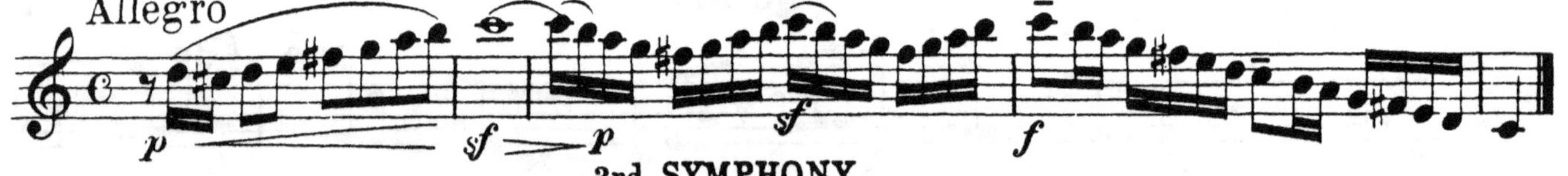

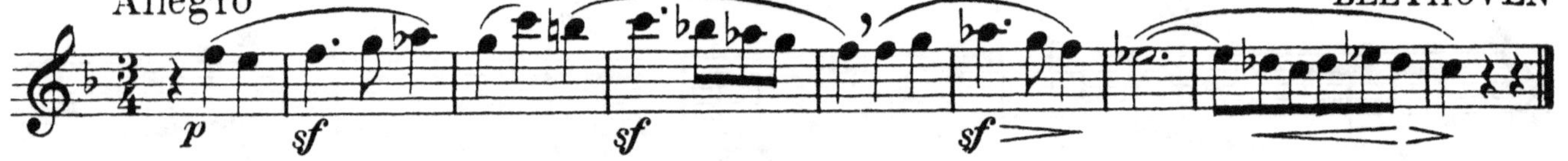

On Accents

REMARK 66. — There are also a number of short and long accents placed above notes to indicate that such notes must be emphasized. However, this accentuation must not be exaggerated, for otherwise they will sound like a *fp* or *sf*. The best manner to play a melodic accent, is by taking off the edge of the attack, starting the note thus: <> with a quick crescendo.

NOTE. — Breath must be taken only where the comma is marked.

Accented Eighth-Notes

On Staccato or Dotted-Notes

REMARK 67.— When a note has a dot above it or the word staccato underneath this means that the note must be played shorter than its value. Eighth notes that are dotted should be played like sixteenths. Quarter and half notes dotted, lose about a quarter of their full value in moderate tempo, however in slow movements they lose only about an eighth of their value.

On Legato-Staccato

REMARK 68.— A legato-staccato consists of playing a number of notes in a half-slurred half-detached manner. The action of the tongue being very smooth as when pronouncing dee-dee. When the last note of a phrase is dotted and tied at the same time to its preceding note, this does not signify, as many think, that the last note must be detached from the foregoing, it is simply intended to cut the last note short (see example marked A). A dash (–) placed over one note denotes that the note must be sustained a little longer than the following notes, Ex. B. If the dash is placed on a number of consecutive notes, this means that the notes be sustained as long as possible, Ex. C.

213. From ♩=88 and up — BERR

Rondo

DE BÉRIOT

(1) Be careful not to slur the last note of the triplet to the following eighth note. Each triplet must stand distinctly apart from the rest.

REMARK 66.— This study is intended to facilitate the passing from the chalumeau to the clarion-register, and vice-versa; it is to be practiced for evenness and not for speed. Do not slide the thumb to the 12th key, but raise slightly the joint of the thumb to manipulate the key.

KLOSÉ

Studies for the High F♯ and G Fingerings

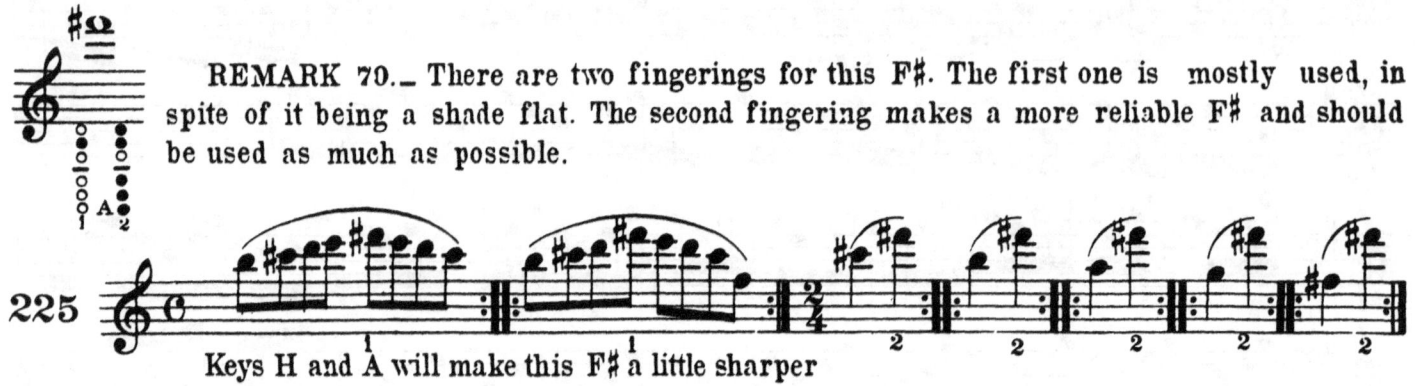

REMARK 70.— There are two fingerings for this F♯. The first one is mostly used, in spite of it being a shade flat. The second fingering makes a more reliable F♯ and should be used as much as possible.

Keys H and A will make this F♯ a little sharper

This G has about ten different fingerings of which we give here the five principal ones; for the others, I refer the clarinetist to the Table of Fingerings.

Fingerings 1 and 2 produce the best G and are used when slurring from any note below the high F to the G.

Fingering J or K is used in G major and minor scales or runs.

Fingering I is used in C major passages

REMARK 71.— When playing in the high register with a B♭ Clarinet, key A may be kept open for notes above the C♯. However, on the A Clarinet, the high register being much sharper in pitch than the B♭ instrument, it is advisable not to use key A.

For notes above the high G, I refer the player to the complete Table of Fingerings in the First Book of this Method.

Scale Studies

REMARK 72. When practising scales the following must constantly be kept in mind: 1.— No note must be played shorter or longer than the other; notes must be linked well together and flow freely and evenly from the instrument. 2.— The tone must be well sustained and rendered as beautiful as possible. 3.— The embouchure must not vacillate but must remain stationary as if playing only one note. 4.— The scales should be memorized and played daily. 5.— Play them at first in a slow tempo and quicken it according to the progress you make.

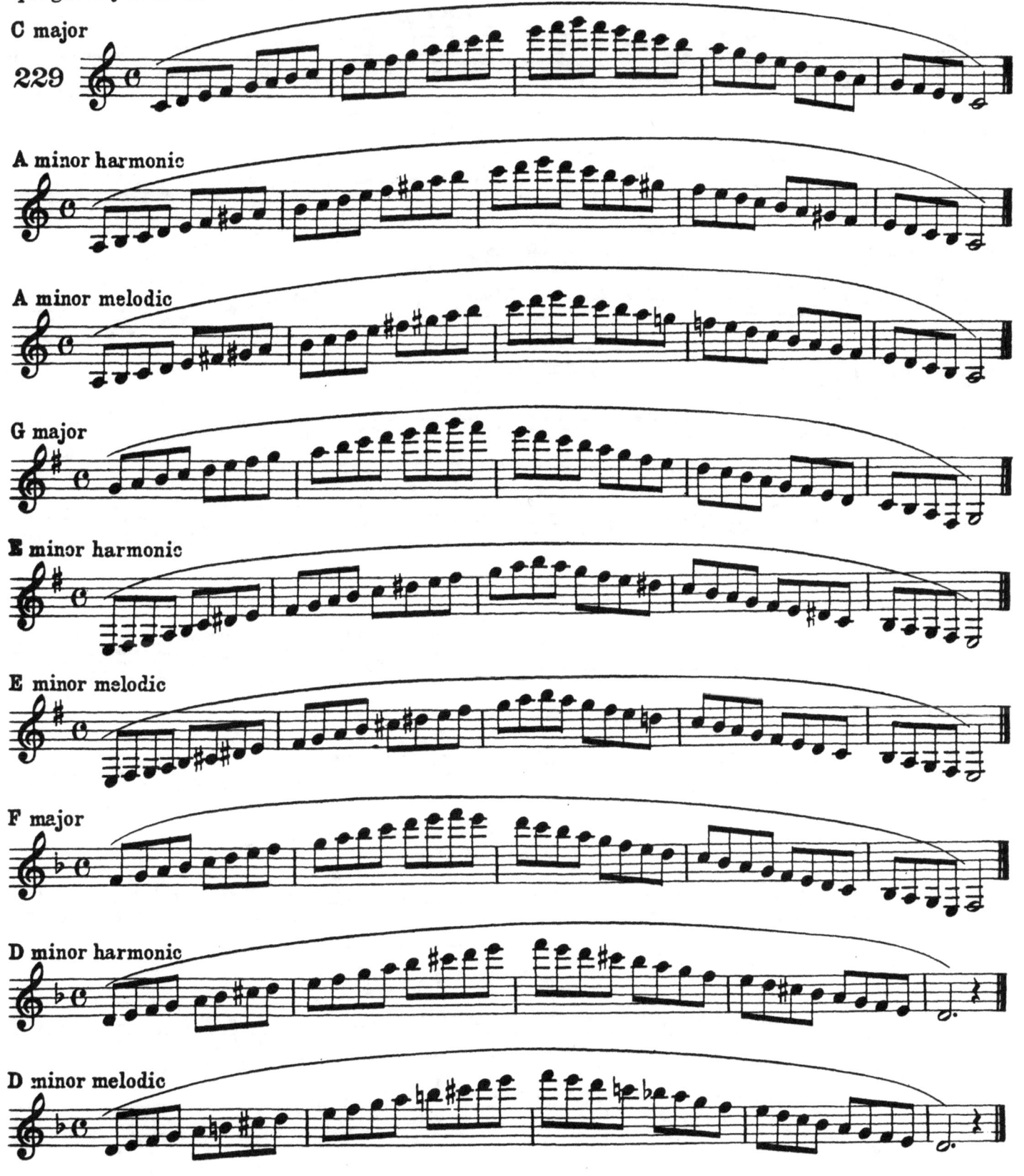

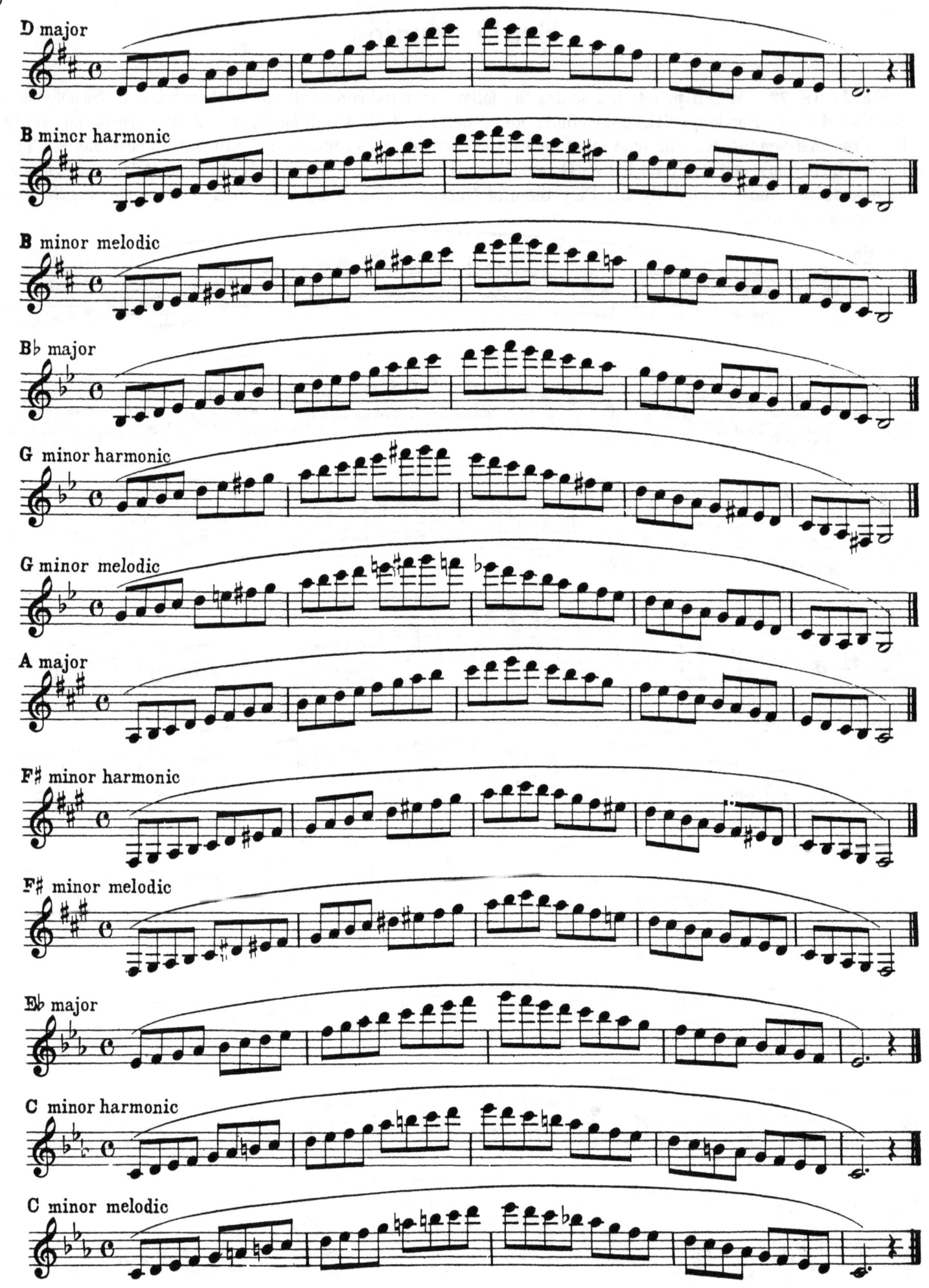

Chromatic-Scale Exercises

Practice study 100 in Tempo di Valse ♩. = 60
Practice study 182 in E major

Practice study 173 in B major. Studies 174 and 175 in F# major.

Practice study **148** in B major; Duet **154** in D♭ major.

Musical Terms

Tempo, as applied here, means "rate of speed." Every composition bears a mark denoting at what speed the music should be played. Italian words are generally used to express the composer's directions. Metronome marks are also often added.

Tempo indications can be divided into three grades. i. e.

1. **Largo**, (slow, solemn)
   Grave, (majestical, weighty)   Larghetto, (less slow than Largo)
   Adagio, (slow, deliberate)

2. **Moderato**, (moderately quick)
   Andante, (going easily)   Andantino, (a little faster than Andante)
   Allegretto, (lightly, cheerfully)

3. **Allegro**, (lively, fast)
   Vivace, (lively, briskly, quickly)   Presto, (rapidly)
   Prestissimo, (very fast)

Each of the above tempo marks has generally an adjective to denote the exact mood in which a composition must be performed. The following are those mostly used.

Largo
- *Assai* (very)
- *Ma non troppo* (not dragging)

Andante
- *Affectuoso* (with much pathos)
- *Cantabile* (in a very singing style)
- *Con moto* (with motion, floating)
- *Grazioso* (with graceful expression)
- *Maestoso* (with majesty)
- *Pastorale* (in a pastoral way)
- *Sostenuto* (in a sustained manner)

Allegretto *Scherzando* (in a playful style)

Adagio *Molto* (very slow)

Allegro
- *Agitato* (quick with agitation)
- *Comodo* (easy going)
- *Con brio* (with brilliancy)
- *Con fuoco* (with fire and animation)
- *Con spirito* (with spirit)
- *Dimolto* (animated)
- *Giusto* (in a steady precise time)
- *Ma non presto* (but not too fast)
- *Risoluto* (vigorous)
- *Veloce* (with velocity)
- *Vivace* (with vivacity)
- *Vivo* (lively)

Music abounds also with such indications as follow:

Musical terms	Abbreviated	Meaning
Accelerando	accel.	growing faster
Ad libitum or / A piacere	ad lib.	at pleasure, the time and expression being left to the performer
Al segno	A. S. 𝄋	return to the sign
Alla breve	₵	¼ measure taken in two beats, half note to each beat
A tempo	a tem.	the same time as the first
Attacca		begin the next movement immediately
Bis		repeat
Con anima or Animato		with animation
Con moto		with motion, rather quick
Crescendo	cresc.	with gradually increasing power of tone
Da Capo	D. C.	from the beginnig
Dal Segno	D. S. 𝄋	repeat from the sign

Decrescendo	decres.	gradually decreasing in power of tone
Diminuendo	dim.	gradually diminishing the tone
Dolce		sweetly, softly, gently
Energico		forcible, vigorous
Espressivo		with feeling
Forte	*f*	loud
Fortissimo	*ff*	very loud
Forzando	*fz*	laying a stress upon one note or chord
Furioso		fierce, vehement
Grandioso		noble, lofty, elevated
Leggiero		light, swift, delicate
Lento		in slow time
L'istesso tempo		like the previous tempo
Loco		the passage to be played as written
Lusingando		coaxing; in a playful, persuasive style
Meno		less
Mosso		movement
Morendo		gradually dying away
Obligato		necessary
Perdendosi		gradually decreasing both tone and time
Più		more
Piano	*p*	soft
Pianissimo	*pp*	very soft
Poco a poco		little by little
Rallentando	rall.	becoming gradually slower
Replica		on each beat
Ritardando	rit.	synonym of rallentando
Ritenuto	rit.	becoming slower, but more abruptly than ritardando
Rinforzando	*rfz*	reinforced
Senza		without
Segue		go on in a like manner
Sempre		always
Simile		similarly, meaning the continuation of some form previously indicated
Smorzando	smorz.	gradually dying away
Solo		music for one principal voice or instrument
Divisi		one performer to each part
Sotto		under, below
Sostenuto	sost.	sustained
Stringendo	string.	accelerating the time
Tacet		be silent
Tenuto	ten.	sustained
Tema		a theme or subject
Tutti		all, the entire band or chorus
Unisono	unis.	two, or more, parts to play in unison
Volto Subito	V. S.	turn the page quickly

The above is by no means a complete list of expression and tempo marks; but only the ones ordinarily encountered, and these, at **least**, the student should understand and remember.